2002

Pray

MW00462589

"Come, Follow Me."

The Word Among Us Press
9639 Doctor Perry Road
Ijamsville, Maryland 21754
www.wau.org
ISBN: 0-932085-53-9

©2001 by The Word Among Us Press
All Rights Reserved

Scripture quotations are from the Revised Standard Version
of the Bible, ©1946, 1952, 1971, by the Division of Christian Education of the
National Council of the Churches of Christ in the U.S.A.
Used by permission.

Scripture readings from the Roman Catholic liturgical calendar are adapted for use in
the United States. Celebration of solemnities, feasts, memorials or other observances
particular to your country, diocese or parish may result in some variation.

Cover design by Christopher Ranck and David Crosson

No part of this publication may be reproduced, stored in a retrieval system, or
transmitted in any form by any means—electronic, mechanical, photocopy, recording
or any other—except for brief quotations in printed reviews, without the prior
permission of the publisher.

Made and printed in Hong Kong

Dear Friends in Christ,

Come, follow me. We know that Jesus spoke these words to Peter and Andrew (Matthew 4:19), to Zebedee's sons James and John (Matthew 21), to Levi (Mark 2:14), and to the rich young man (Luke 18:22). He must have issued the same call to women such as Mary Magdalene, Joanna, and Susanna, who were "with him" and provided for him "out of their resources" (Luke 8:1-3). To men and women throughout the ages, and to us today, Jesus extends a personal invitation to share his life—and to make his teachings our rock and foundation.

Come, follow me. To become a follower of Jesus means to acknowledge, as Peter did, that Jesus is "the Messiah, the Son of the living God" (Matthew 16:16). To be his disciple means to turn to him for salvation, to accept and obey his commandments, and to embrace his will and purpose for our lives. Finally, as Jesus' disciples, we are called to share in his death. *If any want to become my followers, let them deny themselves and take up their cross daily and follow me (Luke 9:23).* We die with Christ so that we might share, too, in his resurrection.

Come, follow me is the theme chosen for our 2002 prayer journal. We cannot follow Jesus in quite the same way his first disciples did—by accompanying him as he went about Galilee, Judea, and Jerusalem preaching and teaching and healing. We can "follow" him, however, as we encounter him personally in our time of prayer and Scripture reading every day. There we can draw near to Jesus, staying close by his side as we worship him and listen to his word. As Fr. Tom Forrest points out in the following article, when Jesus calls us to discipleship, he is inviting us to live with him.

In our daily times of prayer, we enter into conversation with Jesus. As we open our hearts to him, we offer him our love and praise. We tell him of our cares and ask for his forgiveness and healing. We seek his guidance for the choices and decisions that face us each day on life's journey. And in that daily encounter, Jesus reveals his heart to us, comforting and strengthening us with his love, instructing us with his truth, and transforming our lives to reflect his own through the power of his Spirit.

Using a prayer journal can help us to recognize as well as remember God's words and actions in our lives. Writing out Scripture passages that seem to particularly "speak" to us can help us to identify the ways in which God is working over the course of the week or month. Noting of our resolutions can reinforce our commitment to respond to these words. By jotting down our struggles and triumphs or recording our petitions and how God has answered them, we have a tangible record to remind us of God's faithfulness. When we compose our own prayers, we express our deepest longings to the Lord. Simply by writing about our daily challenges, we can better face our circumstances, feelings, and temptations truthfully or detect recurring patterns of sin.

Since a prayer journal is private—an exchange between us and God not meant to be read by others—we don't have to "put up a good front," but can be thoroughly honest. Nor should we worry about our writing style, grammar, or spelling.

The 2002 prayer journal features the Mass readings for each day of the year, which are based on the New American Bible translation. At the top of each page of the journal is a New Testament Scripture verse (from the Revised Standard Version translation) or a quotation from a saint or well-known contemporary Christian. Most of the Scripture verses either express Jesus' call to us to follow him as his disciple or teach us how to live out this call. Many of the quotations highlight this theme as well. Whenever possible, quotations have been selected which correspond to the feast days of the saints or special holy days and seasons in the liturgical year.

Come, follow me. Discipleship entails a costly emptying of self, but Jesus never asks more of us than we can give. We can follow him with confidence, for he has gone this way before us and is there to accompany us each step of our way.

Immediately they left their nets and followed him (Matthew 4:20).

The Word Among Us

"Come, Follow Me."

Becoming Like Our Master

By Father Tom Forrest, C.Ss.R.
International Director of Evangelization 2000

We are called to bring to others the Jesus whom we have come to know. What does it mean to know Jesus? What kind of relationship are we meant to have with the Son of God?

We can see signs of it throughout the gospels, and Jesus speaks of it clearly when he tells the apostles, "Go. . . and make disciples of all nations" (Matthew 28:19). Jesus calls all of us into a master-disciple relationship with himself, and if we are called to make other people into disciples of Jesus, then disciples are what we ourselves have to be.

Well, then, each of us must ask, "What does it mean to be a disciple of Jesus? Am I a disciple?" The word "disciple" is found in the New Testament about 250 times. Clearly, it is a very important concept, a foundational term for understanding our relationship with Jesus. It is worth a little effort to go back 2,000 years to find out what the word signified as it came from the lips of Jesus Christ himself.

An Onlooker or a Follower? The gospels show us that being a disciple of Jesus means more than just hearing him and watching him appreciatively. Crowds of people listened to Jesus, hoping to hear something inspiring and get something from him. But there was a great difference between standing in the crowd and joining the band of his followers.

The difference between being an onlooker in the crowd and being a disciple emerged powerfully when Jesus multiplied bread and fish for a crowd of people who had gathered to hear him preach. Immediately after this miracle, Jesus and the twelve crossed the Sea of Galilee in a boat. They apparently wanted to spend some time alone in prayer and fellowship, so they wanted to distance themselves from the crowd for a little while. The other people, however, were so astonished by the multiplied food that they tracked Jesus down and gathered around him once again. Jesus told them, "I assure you, you are following me not because you have understood the signs I am performing but because you have eaten your fill of bread" (see John 6:26).

Jesus then went on to give the people a very challenging teaching: "Unless you eat the flesh of the Son of man and drink his blood, you have no life in you" (John 6:53). The crowd responded, "This is a hard saying. Who can listen to it?" (6:60). At this point, many broke away from him. They were willing to follow Jesus as long as bread was being handed out. But as soon as there was something hard to believe, they left him.

After they left, Jesus turned to those who remained and asked them, "Will you also go away?" (John 6:67). Peter replied, "Lord, to whom shall we go? You have the words of eternal life" (6:68). That is the difference between being in the crowd and being a disciple. The crowd followed only for the immediate advantage. The disciples followed even when Jesus' words were difficult to understand, even when it cost them something to remain with him.

On another occasion, Jesus brought out this difference when he said, "Not every one who says to me, 'Lord, Lord,' will enter the kingdom of heaven, but he who does the will of my Father who is in heaven" (Matthew 7:21). This is the key difference.

Whose Plan? If we remain in the crowd, we will never really know Jesus; we will not grasp who he is and what he is about. And, consequently, we will not be effective as evangelists—either to our neighbors or to our families. The person in the crowd holds back from Jesus, even while looking for his help. He says, "Jesus, save me—according to my plan. Here is how I would like you to take care of me and save me." On the other hand, the disciple says, "Jesus, lead me according to your plan. Show me how I should live. All I want is to become like you." The people in the crowd only call to Jesus, "Save us from this, save us from that, give us this, give us that."

It is true that the disciple asks for what he needs. But he also prays, "Lord, what do you want of me? I will do whatever you want. I will go wherever you send me." The people in the crowd may rejoice in the kingdom of God, but only the part that is here and now. The disciple prays simply, "Your kingdom come—in your time, in your way."

When Jesus says to us, "Come, follow me," he means, "Come, live with me and learn my way of living." He invites us to become like him.

"Come, Follow Me." In the ancient world, discipleship involved a personal relationship between the master and the disciple. It was a more far-reaching relationship than that between a teacher and a student today. In the time of Christ, a disciple's relationship with his master was very much like his relationship with his own parents. A man respected, loved, and obeyed his parents because he had received his life from them. But it was also understood that the gift of life is useless if you don't know how to live it. So, while the parents gave life, it was the master who opened the way to living that life well. By interpreting God's instruction, the master was supposed to show his disciple how to live. Therefore, for the disciple, the honor due his master was similar to the honor due his parents.

A master's main job was not simply to convey facts. He was not intended to be just a communicator of a body of knowledge. His role was to teach the art of living. What he gave, primarily, was formation, not information. And you can't form someone just by talking to him or her. The master had to open his life to his disciple. He had to show his disciple—through word and deed—how to live.

So, when Jesus calls us to discipleship, he is inviting us to live with him. He is inviting us to learn from his example as well as from his words so that our lives can be formed by him. When he says to us, "Come, follow me," he means, "Come, live with me and learn my way of living." He invites us to become like him.

If we want to learn the way of life that Jesus, our master, teaches, we will have to follow him and serve him with the same attitude that Elisha had toward Elijah.

Reflections of Jesus. On the day of Pentecost, 120 disciples of Jesus were filled with the gift of the Spirit and began to evangelize everyone they could. These men and women built the early church by following Jesus' command to make disciples of all nations. How did they do it? They had become 120 reflections of Jesus. Through his discipleship, and by the power of the Spirit, Jesus had multiplied himself 120 times. That is what we as disciples are called to become—images of the master to such a degree that anyone who meets us meets Jesus in us.

When Jesus' first disciples responded to his call to follow him, they became his servants. This was an important part of the relationship between disciple and master. The master opened his life to his disciples and taught them how to live. The disciples responded by serving their master and accepting his instruction.

"Servant" is just as unpopular a title today as it was in Jesus' day. We would not mind being called "doctor" or "professor." But "servant" sounds too lowly, too difficult, to attract us.

Perhaps we can get a better view of it by looking at the relationship between Elijah and Elisha. Elijah, one of the greatest of the Old Testament prophets, called Elisha to be his disciple. He expressed his call by covering Elisha with his cloak—offering him the protection and strength of his teaching. Elisha arose and went after Elijah and "ministered to him" (1 Kings 19:21). That is, Elisha entered into his service.

Why did Elisha basically become Elijah's slave? Well, if he cooked Elijah's meals, he would see how he ate. If he washed and mended his clothing, he would see how he dressed himself. If he cared for his house, he would see how he treated his possessions. If he was at Elijah's service all day long, he would hear how his master spoke and see how he worked. These were all things that Elisha needed to learn if he was going to become a reflection of his master.

If we want to learn the way of life that Jesus, our master, teaches, we will have to follow him and serve him with the same attitude that Elisha had toward Elijah. Realizing who Jesus is, we will be proud to be known as his servants.

Being a Christian means being "Christ like." God doesn't want us to be Christians just because we had baptismal water poured on us. He wants us to become what the water of baptism signifies—men and women incorporated into Jesus Christ. It is only through our relationship with Jesus that we can become like him. Only he can make us like himself. And he can transform us only as we answer his invitation to live with him and serve him. Then, as we know him and are formed by him, we will be able to fulfill the task he has given us: "Go, make disciples of all nations."

On Discipleship
From the *Catechism of the Catholic Church*

The disciple of Christ must not only keep the faith and live on it, but also profess it, confidently bear witness to it, and spread it. "All however must be prepared to confess Christ before men and to follow him along the way of the Cross, amidst the persecution which the Church never lacks" (Vatican II, *Lumen Gentium*, 42). Service of and witness to the faith are necessary to salvation. "So every one who acknowledges me before men, I also will acknowledge before my Father who is in heaven; but whoever denies me before men, I also will deny before my Father who is in heaven" (Matthew 10:32-33). (1816)

From the beginning, Jesus associated his disciples with his own life, revealed the mystery of the Kingdom to them, and gave them a share in his mission, joy, and sufferings. Jesus spoke of a still more intimate communion between him and those who would follow him: "Abide in me, and I in you. . . . I am the vine, you are the branches" (John 15:4-5). And he proclaimed a mysterious and real communion between his own body and ours: "He who eats my flesh and drinks my blood abides in me, and I in him" (John 6:56). (787)

The transmission of the Christian faith consists primarily in proclaiming Jesus Christ in order to lead others to faith in him. From the beginning, the first disciples burned with the desire to proclaim Christ: "We cannot but speak of what we have seen and heard" (Acts 4:20). And they invite people of every era to enter into the joy of their communion with Christ. (425)

On Discipleship
From *The Dictionary of Biblical Theology*

Jesus specified unique requirements for His disciples:

- **Calling.** To become His disciple, intellectual or even moral aptitudes were not important. What matters is a call, the initiative of which comes from Jesus (Mark 1:17-20; John 1:38-40) and behind Him the Father who "gives" Jesus His disciples (John 6:39; 10:29; 17:6,12).

- **Personal attachment to Christ.** To become a disciple of Jesus it is not required to be a man of superior caliber. Indeed the relation which unites disciple and master is not exclusively, or even primarily, one of an intellectual order. He says to the disciple: "Follow me!" In the gospel the verb follow always expresses attachment to the person of Jesus (Matthew 8:19). To follow Jesus is to sever with the past, with a complete break if it is a question of privileged disciples. To follow Jesus is to fashion one's conduct on His, to listen to His lessons, and to conform one's life to that of the Savior (Mark 8:34; 10:21; John 12:26). They were different from the disciples of the Jewish doctors who, having been instructed in the Law, were able to break away from their master and teach on their own. The disciple of Jesus is not bound to a doctrine but to a person: he cannot leave Him who henceforth is for him more than father and mother (Matthew 10:37; Luke 14:25).

- **Destiny and Dignity.** The disciple of Jesus is, therefore, called to share the very destiny of the master: to carry His cross (Mark 8:34), to drink His cup (Mark 10:38), finally to receive from Him the kingdom (Matthew 19:28; Luke 22:28; John 14:3). Therefore, from this time on, whoever would give him simply a glass of water as a disciple would not lose his reward (Matthew 10:42); on the other hand, what a sin "to scandalize one of these little ones!" (Mark 9:42).

*Taken from The Dictionary of Biblical Theology, Updated Second Edition,
edited by Xavier Leon-Dufour, The Word Among Us Press, 2000.*

A Guide to Prayer

Choose a Time.
Make definite time dedicated only to prayer. Try to make it the best time for prayer you can find.

Choose a Place.
It should be free from distractions.

Enter into Prayer.
Examine your conscience and repent of your sins. (Matthew 5:23-24; 6:14-15; Psalm 51:1-5; Psalm 130)

Accept God's Forgiveness.
Let his mercy cleanse your conscience and lift your guilt. (Romans 8:32; Hebrews 9:14)

Lay Aside Anxieties, Problems, Struggles.
Do not allow your troubles to dominate your time with God; he is Lord of all. (Hebrews 12:1-2)

Open Your Heart to the Truths of the Gospel.
- God created you out of love and loves you always. (Genesis 1:27-31; 1 John 4:10-11)
- God sent Jesus to give us life. (John 3:16; Ephesians 2:4-5)
- Jesus died and rose, conquering sin and death. (Romans 5:12-18; 1 Corinthians 15:22-26)
- Jesus promised to be with us and to send the Holy Spirit. (John 14:16; 14:26; 16:7)

- Jesus intercedes for us in heaven. (Romans 8:34; Hebrews 7:25; 1 John 2:1)
- Jesus is coming again. (Matthew 16:27; 25:34)

Come Before the Presence of the Lord. Praise God.
- He is worthy of all praise. (Psalm 95; 136; 150; Hebrews 13:15; 1 Peter 2:9)
- Express your love and gratitude to our Father, to his Son Jesus, and to the Holy Spirit of Truth.
- Speak with God honestly and from the heart.

Ask Questions.
- Listen actively to God in your heart and mind as your read scripture or kneel before him.
- Reflect on his word (Matthew 7:7-11)
- Dwell in the presence of God.

Intercede with Faith.
- For daily bread; Pray for the world, the church, your friends, family, yourself.
- For forgiveness: As you forgive others.
- For strength for the day and its trials.
- For protection from all evil.

Before Leaving Prayer Write Down:
- What God has shown you.
- What you want to carry into the day and remember so that your prayer will bear fruit.
- What you have prayed for.

Abbreviations of Books of the Bible

Acts Acts of the Apostles

Am Amos

Bar Baruch

1 Chr 1 Chronicles

2 Chr 2 Chronicles

Col Colossians

1 Cor 1 Corinthians

2 Cor 2 Corinthians

Dn Daniel

Dt Deuteronomy

Eccl Ecclesiastes

Eph Ephesians

Est Esther

Ex Exodus

Ez Ezekiel

Ezr Ezra

Gal Galatians

Gn Genesis

Hab Habakkuk

Heb Hebrews

Hg Haggai

Hos Hosea

Is Isaiah

Jas James

Jb Job

Jdt Judith

Jer Jeremiah

Jgs Judges

Jl Joel

Jn John

1 Jn 1 John

2 Jn 2 John

3 Jn 3 John

Jon Jonah

Jos Joshua

Jude Jude

1 Kgs 1 Kings

2 Kgs 2 Kings

Lam Lamentations

Lk Luke

Lv Leviticus

Mal Malachi

1 Mc 1 Maccabees

2 Mc 2 Maccabees

Mi Micah

Mk Mark

Mt Matthew

Na Nahum

Neh Nehemiah

Nm Numbers

Ob Obadiah

Phil Philippians

Phlm Philemon

Prv Proverbs

Ps Psalms

1 Pt 1 Peter

2 Pt 2 Peter

Rom Romans

Ru Ruth

Rv Revelation

Sir Sirach

1 Sm 1 Samuel

2 Sm 2 Samuel

Sg Song of Songs

Tb Tobit

1 Thes 1 Thessalonians

2 Thes 2 Thessalonians

Ti Titus

1 Tm 1 Timothy

2 Tm 2 Timothy

Wis Wisdom

Zec Zechariah

> Mary is more blessed because she embraces faith in Christ than because she conceives the flesh of Christ.
> —St. Augustine

1 Tuesday Blessed Virgin Mary, Mother of God

Nm 6:22-27 **Ps** 67:2-3,5-6,8 **Gal** 4:4-7 **Lk** 2:16-21

Holy Day of Obligation

2 Wednesday Saints Basil the Great and Gregory Nazianzen

1 Jn 2:22-28 **Ps** 98:1,2-4 **Jn** 1:19-28

january

1 2 3 4 5 **6** 7 8 9 10 11 12 **13** 14 15

How sweet is the presence of Jesus in the Eucharist to the longing, harassed soul! It is instant peace, and balm to every wound.

—St. Elizabeth Ann Seton

Thursday
3

1 Jn 2:29–3:6 **Ps** 98:1,3-6 **Jn** 1:29–34

_____
_____
_____
_____
_____
_____
_____
_____
_____
_____
_____
_____
_____
_____

Friday Saint Elizabeth Ann Seton
4

1 Jn 3:7-10 **Ps** 98:1,7-9 **Jn** 1:35-42

_____
_____
_____
_____
_____
_____
_____
_____
_____
_____
_____
_____
_____
_____

16 17 18 19 **20** 21 22 23 24 25 26 **27** 28 29 30 31

The obedience of the star calls us to imitate its humble service: to be servants, as best we can, of the grace that invites all men to find Christ.

5 Saturday Saint John Neumann —St. Leo the Great

1 Jn 3:11-21 **Ps** 100:1-5 **Jn** 1:43-51

6 Sunday Epiphany of the Lord

Is 60:1-6 **Ps** 72:1-2,7-8,10-13 **Eph** 3:2-3a, 5-6 **Mt** 2:1-12

january

1　2　3　4　5　6　7　8　9　10　11　12　**13**　14　15

Repent, for the kingdom of heaven is at hand.

—Matthew 4:17

7 Monday Saint Raymond of Peñafort

1 Jn 3:22—4:6 **Ps** 2:7-8,10-11 **Mt** 4:12-17, 23-25

_____

_____

_____

_____

_____

_____

_____

_____

_____

_____

_____

8 Tuesday

1 Jn 4:7-10 **Ps** 72:1-4,7-8 **Mk** 6:34-44

_____

_____

_____

_____

_____

_____

_____

_____

_____

_____

_____

16 17 18 19 **20** 21 22 23 24 25 26 **27** 28 29 30 31

No man has ever seen God; if we love one another, God abides in us and his love is perfected in us.

—1 John 4:12

9 Wednesday

1 Jn 4:11-18 **Ps** 72:1-2,10,12-13 **Mk** 6:45-52

_____
_____
_____
_____
_____
_____
_____
_____
_____
_____
_____

10 Thursday

1 Jn 4:19-5:4 **Ps** 72:1-2,14-15,17 **Lk** 4:14-22a

_____
_____
_____
_____
_____
_____
_____
_____
_____
_____
_____

january

1   2   3   4   5   6   7   8   9   10   11   12   **13**   14   15

> God gives his gifts where he finds the vessel empty enough to receive them.
>
> —C. S. Lewis

11 Friday

1 Jn 5:5-13 **Ps** 147:12-15,19-20 **Lk** 5:12-16

_____
_____
_____
_____
_____
_____
_____
_____
_____
_____
_____

12 Saturday

1 Jn 5:14-21 **Ps** 149:1-6,9 **Jn** 3:22-30

_____
_____
_____
_____
_____
_____
_____
_____
_____
_____
_____

16 17 18 19 **20** 21 22 23 24 25 26 **27** 28 29 30 31

Christ is bathed in light; let us also be bathed in light. Christ is baptized; let us also go down with him, and rise with him.

—St. Gregory Nazianzen

13 Sunday Baptism of the Lord

Is 42:1-4, 6-7 **Ps** 29:1-4,9-10 **Acts** 10:34-38 **Mt** 3:13-17

_____

_____

_____

_____

_____

_____

_____

_____

_____

_____

_____

14 Monday

1 Sm 1:1-8 **Ps** 116:12-14,17-19 **Mk** 1:14-20

_____

_____

_____

_____

_____

_____

_____

_____

_____

_____

_____

_____

january

1 2 3 4 5 **6** 7 8 9 10 11 12 **13** 14 15

If any one serves me, he must follow me; and where I am, there shall my servant be also; if any one serves me, the Father will honor him. —John 12:26

15 Tuesday

1 Sm 1:9-20 **(Ps) 1 Sm** 2:1,4-8 **Mk** 1:21b-28

_____
_____
_____
_____
_____
_____
_____
_____
_____
_____
_____
_____

16 Wednesday

1 Sm 3:1-10, 19-20 **Ps** 40:2-5,7-10 **Mk** 1:29-39

_____
_____
_____
_____
_____
_____
_____
_____
_____
_____
_____
_____

16 17 18 19 **20** 21 22 23 24 25 26 **27** 28 29 30 31

He who knows himself knows all men. He who can love himself, loves all men.

—St. Anthony of Egypt

17 Thursday Saint Anthony

1 Sm 4:1-11 **Ps** 44:10-11,14-15,25-26 **Mk** 1:40-45

18 Friday

1 Sm 8:4-7, 10-22a **Ps** 89:16-19 **Mk** 2:1-12

January

1 2 3 4 5 **6** 7 8 9 10 11 12 **13** 14 15

Do you not know that God's kindness is meant to lead you to repentance?

—Romans 2:4

19 Saturday

1 Sm 9:1-4, 17-19; 10:1a **Ps** 21:2-7 **Mk** 2:13-17

_____

_____

_____

_____

_____

_____

_____

_____

_____

_____

20 Sunday

Is 49:3, 5-6 **Ps** 40:2,4,7-10 **1 Cor** 1:1-3 **Jn** 1:29-34

_____

_____

_____

_____

_____

_____

_____

_____

_____

_____

16 17 18 19 **20** 21 22 23 24 25 26 **27** 28 29 30 31

Christk will guard his own.

—St. Agnes

21 Monday Saint Agnes

1 Sm 15:16-23 **Ps** 50:8-9,16-17,21,23 **Mk** 2:18-22

_____

_____

_____

_____

_____

_____

_____

_____

_____

_____

_____

22 Tuesday Saint Vincent

1 Sm 16:1-13 **Ps** 89:20-22,27-28 **Mk** 2:23-28

_____

_____

_____

_____

_____

_____

_____

_____

_____

_____

_____

_____

january

1 2 3 4 5 **6** 7 8 9 10 11 12 **13** 14 15

We must fear God out of love, not love him out of fear.

—St. Francis de Sales

23 Wednesday

1 Sm 17:32-33, 37, 40-51 **Ps** 144:1-2,9-10 **Mk** 3:1-6

24 Thursday Saint Francis de Sales

1 Sm 18:6-9; 19:1-7 **Ps** 56:2-3,9-14 **Mk** 3:7-12

16 17 18 19 **20** 21 22 23 24 25 26 **27** 28 29 30 31

Guard the truth that has been entrusted to you by the Holy Spirit who dwells within us.

—2 Timothy 1:14

25 Friday Conversion of Saint Paul

Acts 22:3-16 or **Acts** 9:1-22 **Ps** 117:1-2 **Mk** 16:15-18

_____

_____

_____

_____

_____

_____

_____

_____

_____

_____

26 Saturday Saints Timothy and Titus

2 Tm 1:1-8 or **Ti** 1:1-5 **Ps** 23:1-6 **Mk** 3:20-21

_____

_____

_____

_____

_____

_____

_____

_____

_____

_____

_____

january

1 2 3 4 5 **6** 7 8 9 10 11 12 **13** 14 15

To love God is something greater than to know him.

—St. Thomas Aquinas

27 Sunday

Is 8:23-9:3 **Ps** 27:1,4,13-14 **1 Cor** 1:10-13, 17 **Mt** 4:12-23

_____
_____
_____
_____
_____
_____
_____
_____
_____
_____
_____
_____

28 Monday Saint Thomas Aquinas

2 Sm 5:1-7, 10 **Ps** 89:20-22,25-26 **Mk** 3:22-30

_____
_____
_____
_____
_____
_____
_____
_____
_____
_____
_____
_____

16 17 18 19 **20** 21 22 23 24 25 26 **27** 28 29 30 31

All things are possible to him who believes.

—Mark 9:23

29 Tuesday
2 Sm 6:12b-15, 17-19 **Ps** 24:7-10 **Mk** 3:31-35

30 Wednesday
2 Sm 7:4-17 **Ps** 89:4-5,27-30 **Mk** 4:1-20

january

1 2 3 4 5 **6** 7 8 9 10 11 12 **13** 14 15

See that no one finds you motivated by impetuosity or willfulness.

—St. John Bosco

31 Thursday Saint John Bosco

2 Sm 7:18-19, 24-29 **Ps** 132:1-5,11-14 **Mk** 4:21-25

I am the light of the world; he who follows me will not walk in darkness, but will have the light of life.

—John 8:12

january

1 2 3 4 5 **6** 7 8 9 10 11 12 **13** 14 15

If we love God and are faithful to him, we shall be at peace and this peace will endure.

—St. Madeleine Sophie Barat

_____

_____

_____

_____

_____

_____

_____

_____

_____

_____

_____

_____

_____

_____

_____

_____

_____

_____

_____

_____

_____

_____

_____

_____

16　17　18　19　**20**　21　22　23　24　25　26　**27**　28　29　30　31

Repent therefore, and turn again, that your sins may be blotted out, that times of refreshing may come from the presence of the Lord.

—Acts 3:19

1 Friday

2 Sm 11:1-4a,5-10a,13-17 **Ps** 51:3-7,10-11 **Mk** 4:26-34

2 Saturday Presentation of the Lord

Mal 3:1-4 **Ps** 24:7-10 **Heb** 2:14-18 **Lk** 2:22-40

february

1 2 **3** 4 5 6 7 8 9 **10** 11 12 13 14 15

Blessed are the pure in heart, for they shall see God.

—Matthew 5:8

3 Sunday

Zep 2:3; 3:12-13 Ps 146:6-10 **1 Cor** 1:26-31 **Mt** 5:1-12a

_____

_____

_____

_____

_____

_____

_____

_____

_____

_____

_____

4 Monday

2 Sm 15:13-14,30; 16:5-13a **Ps** 3:2-7 **Mk** 5:1-20

_____

_____

_____

_____

_____

_____

_____

_____

_____

_____

_____

16 **17** 18 19 20 21 22 23 **24** 25 26 27 28

The more you pray, the easier it becomes. The easier it becomes, the more you'll pray.

—Mother Teresa of Calcutta

5 Tuesday Saint Agatha

2 Sm 18:9-10,14b,24–25a,30–19:3 **Ps** 86:1-6 **Mk** 5:21-43

6 Wednesday Saint Paul Miki

2 Sm 24:2,9-17 **Ps** 32:1-2,5-7 **Mk** 6:1-6

february

1 2 **3** 4 5 6 7 8 9 **10** 11 12 13 14 15

Our goal is God, the source of all good. . . We are to place our trust in God and in no one else.

—St. Jerome Emiliani

7 Thursday

1 Kgs 2:1-4,10-12 (**Ps**) **1 Chr** 29:10-12 **Mk** 6:7-13

8 Friday Saint Jerome Emiliani

Sir 47:2-11 **Ps** 18:31,47,50-51 **Mk** 6:14-29

16 **17** 18 19 20 21 22 23 **24** 25 26 27 28

Let your light so shine before men, that they may see your good works and give glory to your Father in heaven.

—Matthew 5:16

9 Saturday

1 Kgs 3:4-13 Ps 119:9-14 Mk 6:30-34

10 Sunday

Is 58:7-10 Ps 112:4-9 1 Cor 2:1-5 Mt 5:13-16

february

1 2 **3** 4 5 6 7 8 9 **10** 11 12 13 14 15

Mary is so beautiful that to see her again one would be
willing to die.

—St. Bernadette Soubirous

11 Monday Our Lady of Lourdes

1 Kgs 8:1-7,9-13 **Ps** 132:6-10 **Mk** 6:53-56

12 Tuesday

1 Kgs 8:22-23,27-30 **Ps** 84:3-5,10-11 **Mk** 7:1-13

16 **17** 18 19 20 21 22 23 **24** 25 26 27 28

Jesus Christ himself is the most sublime grace of the whole of Lent. It is he who presents himself to us in all the wonderful simplicity of the Gospel. —Pope John Paul II

13 Wednesday Ash Wednesday

Jl 2:12-18 **Ps** 51:3-6,12-14,17 **2 Cor** 5:20–6:2 **Mt** 6:1-6,16-18

14 Thursday Saints Cyril and Methodius

Dt 30:15-20 **Ps** 1:1-4,6 **Lk** 9:22-25

february

1 2 **3** 4 5 6 7 8 9 **10** 11 12 13 14 15

Give Christ free entrance into your heart, and keep out all things that withstand his entrance.

—Thomas à Kempis

15 Friday

Is 58:1-9a **Ps** 51:3-6,18-19 **Mt** 9:14-15

16 Saturday

Is 58:9b-14 **Ps** 86:1-6 **Lk** 5:27-32

16 **17** 18 19 20 21 22 23 **24** 25 26 27 28

If any one is in Christ, he is a new creation; the old has passed away, behold, the new has come.

—2 Corinthians 5:17

17 First Sunday of Lent

Gn 2:7-9; 3:1-7 **Ps** 51:3-6,12-14,17 **Rom** 5:12-19 **Mt** 4:1-11

18 Monday

Lv 19:1-2,11-18 **Ps** 19:8-10,15 **Mt** 25:31-46

february

1 2 **3** 4 5 6 7 8 9 **10** 11 12 13 14 15

The best-used hour in our lives is that in which we love Jesus most.

—Charles de Foucauld

19 Tuesday

Is 55:10-11   **Ps** 34:4-7,16-19   **Mt** 6:7-15

_____

_____

_____

_____

_____

_____

_____

_____

_____

_____

_____

20 Wednesday

Jon 3:1-10   **Ps** 51:3-4,12-13,18-19   **Lk** 11:29-32

_____

_____

_____

_____

_____

_____

_____

_____

_____

_____

_____

16 **17** 18 19 20 21 22 23 **24** 25 26 27 28

Let your understanding strengthen your patience. In serenity look forward to the joy that follows sadness.

—St. Peter Damian

21 Thursday Saint Peter Damian
Est C:12,14–16,23–25 **Ps** 138:1–3,7–8 **Mt** 7:7–12

22 Friday Chair of St. Peter
1 Pt 5:1-4 **Ps** 23:1-6 **Mt** 16:13-19

february

1 2 **3** 4 5 6 7 8 9 **10** 11 12 13 14 15

Eighty-six years I have served him and he never did me wrong;
how can I blaspheme my King and Savior?

—St. Polycarp

23 Saturday Saint Polycarp

Dt 26:16-19 **Ps** 119:1-2,4-5,7-8 **Mt** 5:43-48

24 Second Sunday of Lent

Gn 12:1-4a **Ps** 33:4-5,18-20,22 **2 Tm** 1:8b-10 **Mt** 17:1-9

16 **17** 18 19 20 21 22 23 **24** 25 26 27 28

The wages of sin is death, but the free gift of God is eternal life in Christ Jesus our Lord.

—Romans 6:23

25 Monday

Dn 9:4b–10 **Ps** 79:8-9,11,13 **Lk** 6:36-38

The darkness is a place of growth
"Sophia"

26 Tuesday

Is 1:10,16–20 **Ps** 50:8-9,16-17,21,23 **Mt** 23:1-12

february

1 2 **3** 4 5 6 7 8 9 **10** 11 12 13 14 15

The fruit of the Spirit is love, joy, peace, patience, kindness, goodness, faithfulness, gentleness, self-control.

27 Wednesday

Jer 18:18-20 **Ps** 31:5-6,14-16 **Mt** 20:17-28

_____

_____

_____

_____

_____

_____

_____

_____

_____

_____

_____

_____

28 Thursday

Jer 17:5-10 **Ps** 1:1-4,6 **Lk** 16:19-31

_____

_____

_____

_____

_____

_____

_____

_____

_____

_____

_____

_____

16 **17** 18 19 20 21 22 23 **24** 25 26 27 28

In our own life we must reproduce Christ's life. We need to come to know him by reading and meditating on Scripture.

—Blessed Josemariá Escrivá

february

1 2 **3** 4 5 6 7 8 9 **10** 11 12 13 14 15

Forgetting what lies behind and straining forward to what lies ahead, I press on toward the goal for the prize of the upward call of God in Christ Jesus.

—Philippians 3:13-14

_____

_____

_____

_____

_____

_____

_____

_____

_____

_____

_____

_____

_____

_____

_____

_____

_____

_____

_____

_____

_____

_____

_____

_____

16 **17** 18 19 20 21 22 23 **24** 25 26 27 28

> Nothing done in God's will is done in vain on this earth.

> —Pope John XXIII

1 Friday

Gn 37:3–4,12–13a,17b–28 **Ps** 105:16–21 **Mt** 21:33–43,45–46

2 Saturday

Mi 7:14–15,18–20 **Ps** 103:1–4,9–12 **Lk** 15:1–3,11–32

march

1 2 **3** 4 5 6 7 8 9 **10** 11 12 13 14 15

Since God is perfect in loving man, man must be perfect in loving his neighbor.
—St. Vincent Pallotti

3 Third Sunday of Lent

Ex 17:3-7 Ps 95:1-2,6-9 **Rom** 5:1-2,5-8 **Jn** 4:5-42

_____
_____
_____
_____
_____
_____
_____
_____
_____
_____
_____
_____

4 Monday Saint Casimir

2 Kgs 5:1-15a **Ps** 42:2-3; 43:3-4 **Lk** 4:24-30

_____
_____
_____
_____
_____
_____
_____
_____
_____
_____
_____
_____

16 **17** 18 19 20 21 22 23 **24** 25 26 27 28 29 30 **31**

Be merciful, even as your Father is merciful.

—Luke 6:36

5 Tuesday

Dn 3:25,34-43 **Ps** 25:4-9 **Mt** 18:21-35

6 Wednesday

Dt 4:1,5-9 **Ps** 147:12-13,15-16,19-20 **Mt** 5:17-19

march

1 2 **3** 4 5 6 7 8 9 **10** 11 12 13 14 15

If we share with the poor, out of love for God, we shall receive according to his promise a hundredfold in eternal happiness.

—St. John of God

7 Thursday Saints Perpetua and Felicity

Jer 7:23-28 **Ps** 95:1-2,6-9 **Lk** 11:14-23

8 Friday St. John of God

Hos 14:2-10 **Ps** 81:6-11,14,17 **Mk** 12:28b-34

16 **17** 18 19 20 21 22 23 **24** 25 26 27 28 29 30 **31**

Hope everything from the mercy of God. It is as boundless as his power.

—St. Frances of Rome

9 Saturday Saint Frances of Rome

Hos 6:1-6 **Ps** 51:3-4,18-21 **Lk** 18:9-14

_____

_____

_____

_____

_____

_____

_____

_____

_____

_____

10 Fourth Sunday of Lent

1 Sm 16:1b,6-7,10-13a **Ps** 23:1-6 **Eph** 5:8-14 **Jn** 9:1-41

_____

_____

_____

_____

_____

_____

_____

_____

_____

_____

march

1 2 **3** 4 5 6 7 8 9 **10** 11 12 13 14 15

Make love your aim.

—1 Corinthians 14:1

11 Monday

Is 65:17–21 **Ps** 30:2,4–6,11–13 **Jn** 4:43–54

_____
_____
_____
_____
_____
_____
_____
_____
_____
_____

12 Tuesday

Ez 47:1–9,12 **Ps** 46:2–3,5–6,8–9 **Jn** 5:1–16

_____
_____
_____
_____
_____
_____
_____
_____
_____

16 **17** 18 19 20 21 22 23 **24** 25 26 27 28 29 30 **31**

True charity means returning good for evil—always.

—St. Mary Mazzarello

13 Wednesday

Is 49:8-15 **Ps** 145:8-9,13-14,17-18 **Jn** 5:17-30

14 Thursday

Ex 32:7-14 **Ps** 106:19-23 **Jn** 5:31-47

march

1 2 **3** 4 5 6 7 8 9 **10** 11 12 13 14 15

We have to win heaven with our ordinary work. We need, then, to try to imitate Jesus whose labor with his hands greatly ennobled the dignity of work.

—Gaudium et spes, Vatican II

15 Friday

Wis 2:1a,12-22 **Ps** 34:17-21,23 **Jn** 7:1-2,10,25-30

16 Saturday

Jer 11:18-20 **Ps** 7:2-3,9-12 **Jn** 7:40-53

I am the resurrection and the life; he who believes in me, though he die, yet shall he live.

—John 11:25

17 Fifth Sunday of Lent

Ez 37:12-14 **Ps** 130:1-8 **Rom** 8:8-11 **Jn** 11:1-45

18 Monday Saint Cyril of Jerusalem

Dn 13:1-9,15-17,19-30, 33-62 **Ps** 23:1-6 **Jn** 8:1-11

march

1 2 **3** 4 5 6 7 8 9 **10** 11 12 13 14 15

Imitate St. Joseph by beginning your day's work with God, and ending it for him.

—St. John Vianney

19 Tuesday Saint Joseph, husband of the Blessed Virgin Mary

2 Sm 7:4–5a,12–14a,16 **Ps** 89:2–5,27,29 **Rom** 4:13,16–18,22

Mt 1:16,18–21,24a or **Lk** 2:41–51a

20 Wednesday

Dn 3:14–20,91–92,95 **(Ps) Dn** 3:52–56 **Jn** 8:31–42

16 **17** 18 19 20 21 22 23 **24** 25 26 27 28 29 30 **31**

Be kind to one another, tenderhearted, forgiving one another, as
God in Christ forgave you.

—Ephesians 4:32

21 Thursday

Gn 17:3-9 **Ps** 105:4-9 **Jn** 8:51-59

22 Friday

Jer 20:10-13 **Ps** 18:2-7 **Jn** 10:31-42

march

1 2 **3** 4 5 6 7 8 9 **10** 11 12 13 14 15

The more we empty ourselves, the more we will be able to be filled with God.

—Mother Teresa of Calcutta

23 Saturday Saint Toribio de Mogrovejo

Ez 37:21-28 (Ps) Jer 31:10-13 Jn 11:45-57

24 Palm Sunday

Mt 21:1-11 Is 50:4-7 Ps 22:8-9,17-20,23-24 Phil 2:6-11

Mt 26:14–27:66

16 **17** 18 19 20 21 22 23 **24** 25 26 27 28 29 30 **31**

A new commandment I give to you, that you love one another; even as I have loved you, that you also love one another.

—John 13:34

25 Monday of Holy Week

Is 42:1-7 **Ps** 27:1-3,13-14 **Jn** 12:1-11

26 Tuesday of Holy Week

Is 49:1-6 **Ps** 71:1-6,15,17 **Jn** 13:21-33,36-38

march

1 2 **3** 4 5 6 7 8 9 **10** 11 12 13 14 15

By this we know love, that he laid down his life for us; and we ought to lay down our lives for the brethren.

—1 John 3:16

27 Wednesday of Holy Week

Is 50:4-9a **Ps** 69:8-10,21-22,31,33-34 **Mt** 26:14-25

_____

_____

_____

_____

_____

_____

_____

_____

_____

_____

28 Holy Thursday

Ex 12:1-8,11-14 **Ps** 116:12-13,15-18 **1 Cor** 11:23-26 **Jn** 13:1-15

_____

_____

_____

_____

_____

_____

_____

_____

_____

_____

16 **17** 18 19 20 21 22 23 **24** 25 26 27 28 29 30 **31**

The central Christian belief is that Christ's death has somehow put us right with God and given us a fresh start.

—C. S. Lewis

29 Good Friday

Is 52:13–53:12 **Ps** 31:2,6,12-13,15-17,25 **Heb** 4:14-16; 5:7-9

Jn 18:1–19:42

30 Holy Saturday (Easter Vigil)

Gn 1:1–2:2 **Gn** 22:1-18 **Ex** 14:15–15:1 **Is** 54:5-14 **Is** 55:1-11

Bar 3:9-15,32–4:4 **Ez** 36:16-17a,18-28 **Rom** 6:3-11 **Mt** 28:1-10

march

1 2 **3** 4 5 6 7 8 9 **10** 11 12 13 14 15

Let all heaven burst with joy! Let all earth resound with gladness!
For Christ is risen: Christ, our lasting joy! Christ has risen from
the dead!   —St. John of Damascus

31 Easter Sunday

Acts 10:34a,37-43 **Ps** 118:1-2,16-17,22-23 **Col** 3:1-4

Jn 20:1-9

16 **17** 18 19 20 21 22 23 **24** 25 26 27 28 29 30 **31**

If then you have been raised with Christ, seek the things that are above, where Christ is, seated at the right hand of God.

—Colossians 3:1

march

1   2   **3**   4   5   6   7   8   9   **10**   11   12   13   14   15

Dear Friend in Christ,

At *The Word Among Us*, we value your opinion. We would be grateful to you if you would take a moment and tell us what you think of the 2002 Prayer Journal. Our hope is that we can continue to make the Prayer Journal a useful tool for you to grow in your love for Jesus. In gratitude for your completed survey, we will take $1 off the price of the Prayer Journal for the year 2003! Just send this survey in, and we will reserve your copy of next year's Prayer Journal with a $1 discount.

Please check the statements that most reflect your opinions:

1) I find that the quotes from the saints and the psalms are:

   Enjoyable and inspirational ____

   Not enjoyable and inspirational ____   I have no opinion ____

2) If I could add anything to the quotes or readings, it would be:

   _____

   _____

   _____

3) I believe the amount of space provided for daily journaling is:

   Just right ____   Too much ____   Not Enough ____

4) I think the overall quality of the Prayer Journal is:

   Excellent____   Very Good ____   Good ____   Average ____

   Not Good _____

5) Would you want each day to have its own page for daily journaling even if the cost of the journal increased by $2.00?

   ____ Yes, I agree   ____ No, I disagree

   ____ I have no opinion

6) Do you use the companion to the Prayer Journal, *Abide in My Word: Mass Readings at Your Fingertips*?

☐ Yes   ☐ No

7) If I could change or improve the Prayer Journal for next year, I would:

_____

_____

_____

Thank you for completing our survey. To reserve next year's Journal at the reduced price, complete the form below and return to:

Prayer Journal Survey
The Word Among Us
9639 Doctor Perry Road, #126N
Ijamsville, MD 21754-9900

☐ **YES!** Reserve _____ copies of next year's Prayer Journal. **I understand that I will receive $1 off each copy and therefore only pay $11.95 plus $4 shipping and handling. I will not be billed until I receive the 2003 Prayer Journal in the Fall of 2002.**

Name _____

Address _____

City _____

State _____ Zip _____

Country _____

Phone (_____) _____

email: _____

NOTE: Only surveys returned by <u>May 31, 2002</u> will be eligible for this discount.

QUESTIONS? Call *The Word Among Us* Customer Service at 1-800-775-WORD (9673) if you have any questions about this discount offer.   SJPØ3

To him who sits upon the throne and to the Lamb be blessing and honor and glory and might for ever and ever!

—Revelation 5:13

The Resurrection of Jesus is the crowning truth of our
faith in Christ.   —Catechism of the Catholic Church

1 Monday

Acts 2:14,22-33 **Ps** 16:1-2,5,7-11 **Mt** 28:8-15

2 Tuesday

Acts 2:36-41 **Ps** 33:4-5,18-20,22 **Jn** 20:11-18

april

1 2 3 4 5 6 **7** 8 9 10 11 12 13 **14** 15

Our commonwealth is in heaven, and from it we await a Savior, the Lord Jesus Christ, who will change our lowly body to be like his glorious body.

—Philippians 3:20-21

3 Wednesday

Acts 3:1-10 **Ps** 105:1-4,6-9 **Lk** 24:13-35

---

4 Thursday

Acts 3:11-26 **Ps** 8:2,5-9 **Lk** 24:35-48

---

16 17 18 19 20 **21** 22 23 24 25 26 27 **28** 29 30

Go into all the world and preach the gospel to the whole creation.

—Mark 16:15

5 Friday

Acts 4:1-12 Ps 118:1-2,4,22-27 Jn 21:1-14

6 Saturday

Acts 4:13-21 Ps 118:1,14-21 Mk 16:9-15

april

1 2 3 4 5 6 **7** 8 9 10 11 12 13 **14** 15

Let us imitate the great humility of the most holy Virgin.

—St. Teresa of Avila

7 Sunday

Acts 2:42-47 **Ps** 118:2-4,13-15,22-24 **1 Pt** 1:3-9 **Jn** 20:19-31

_____

_____

_____

_____

_____

_____

_____

_____

_____

_____

_____

8 Monday Annunciation of the Lord

Is 7:10-14; 8:10 **Ps** 40:7-11 **Heb** 10:4-10 **Lk** 1:26-38

_____

_____

_____

_____

_____

_____

_____

_____

_____

_____

_____

16 17 18 19 20 **21** 22 23 24 25 26 27 **28** 29 30

To receive God's grace into our hearts they must be emptied of our own vainglory.

—St. Francis de Sales

9 Tuesday

Acts 4:32-37 **Ps** 93:1-2,5 **Jn** 3:7b-15

10 Wednesday

Acts 5:17-26 **Ps** 34:2-9 **Jn** 3:16-21

april

1 2 3 4 5 6 **7** 8 9 10 11 12 13 **14** 15

If you set out to meet God, he will come to meet you.

—St. John Vianney

11 Thursday Saint Stanislaus

Acts 5:27-33 Ps 34:2,9,17-20 Jn 3:31-36

12 Friday

Acts 5:34-42 Ps 27:1,4,13-14 Jn 6:1-15

16 17 18 19 20 **21** 22 23 24 25 26 27 **28** 29 30

God is light and in him is no darkness at all.

—1 John 1:5

13 Saturday Saint Martin I
Acts 6:1-7 **Ps** 33:1-2,4-5,18-19 **Jn** 6:16-21

14 Sunday
Acts 2:14,22-33 **Ps** 16:1-2,5,7-11 **1 Pt** 1:17-21 **Lk** 24:13-35

april

1 2 3 4 5 6 **7** 8 9 10 11 12 13 **14** 15

> I am the bread of life; he who comes to me shall not hunger, and he who believes in me shall never thirst.
>
> —John 6:35

15 Monday

Acts 6:8-15 **Ps** 119:23-24,26-27,29-30 **Jn** 6:22-29

_____

_____

_____

_____

_____

_____

_____

_____

_____

_____

_____

16 Tuesday

Acts 7:51–8:1a **Ps** 31:3-4,6-8,17,21 **Jn** 6:30-35

_____

_____

_____

_____

_____

_____

_____

_____

_____

_____

_____

16 17 18 19 20 **21** 22 23 24 25 26 27 **28** 29 30

Believe in God with all your might, for hope rests on faith, love on hope, and victory on love.

—Nicholas of Flue

17 Wednesday

Acts 8:1b-8 **Ps** 66:1-7 **Jn** 6:35-40

18 Thursday

Acts 8:26-40 **Ps** 66:8-9,16-17,20 **Jn** 6:44-51

april

1 2 3 4 5 6 **7** 8 9 10 11 12 13 **14** 15

Let all that you do be done in love.

—1 Corinthians 16:14

19 Friday
Acts 9:1-20 **Ps** 117:1-2 **Jn** 6:52-59

20 Saturday
Acts 9:31-42 **Ps** 116:12-17 **Jn** 6:60-69

16 17 18 19 20 **21** 22 23 24 25 26 27 **28** 29 30

The Son of man came to seek and to save the lost.

—Luke 19:10

21 Sunday

Acts 2:14a,36-41 **Ps** 23:1-6 **1 Pt** 2:20b-25 **Jn** 10:1-10

22 Monday

Acts 11:1-18 **Ps** 42:2-3; 43:3-4 **Jn** 10:11-18

april

1 2 3 4 5 6 **7** 8 9 10 11 12 13 **14** 15

God is more anxious to bestow his blessings on us than we are to receive them.

—St. Augustine

23 Tuesday Saint George; Saint Adalbert

Acts 11:19-26 **Ps** 87:1-7 **Jn** 10:22-30

24 Wednesday Saint Fidelis of Sigmaringen

Acts 12:24–13:5a **Ps** 67:2-3,5-6,8 **Jn** 12:44-50

16 17 18 19 20 **21** 22 23 24 25 26 27 **28** 29 30

I am the way, and the truth, and the life.

—John 14:6

25 Thursday Saint Mark the Evangelist
1 Pt 5:5b-14 **Ps** 89:2-3,6-7,16-17 **Mk** 16:15-20

_____

_____

_____

_____

_____

_____

_____

_____

_____

_____

_____

26 Friday
Acts 13:26-33 **Ps** 2:6-11 **Jn** 14:1-6

_____

_____

_____

_____

_____

_____

_____

_____

_____

_____

_____

april

1 2 3 4 5 6 **7** 8 9 10 11 12 13 **14** 15

The mind of the Scriptures can never be exhausted. It is a well
without a bottom.
—St. John Chrysostom

27 Saturday *Tuesday 2010*
Acts 13:44-52 Ps 98:1-4 Jn 14:7-14

cloudy

28 Sunday *Wednesday 2010*
Acts 6:1-7 Ps 33:1-2,4-5,18-19 1 Pt 2:4-9 Jn 14:1-12

Cloudy —

16 17 18 19 20 **21** 22 23 24 25 26 27 **28** 29 30

You, God, are a fire ever burning and never consumed, which itself consumes all the selfish love that fills my being.

—St. Catherine of Siena

29 **Monday** Saint Catherine of Siena

Acts 14:5-18 **Ps** 115:1-4,15-16 **Jn** 14:21-26

30 **Tuesday** Saint Pius V

Acts 14:19-28 **Ps** 145:10-13,21 **Jn** 14:27-31a

april

1 2 3 4 5 6 **7** 8 9 10 11 12 13 **14** 15

Since we are justified by faith, we have peace with God through our Lord Jesus Christ.

—Romans 5:1

_____

_____

_____

_____

_____

_____

_____

_____

_____

_____

_____

_____

_____

_____

_____

_____

_____

_____

_____

_____

_____

_____

_____

_____

_____

_____

16 17 18 19 20 **21** 22 23 24 25 26 27 **28** 29 30

By dying for others, the Word banished death for all mankind.
—St. Athanasius

1 Wednesday Saint Joseph the Worker
Acts 15:1-6 **Ps** 122:1-5 **Jn** 15:1-8

2 Thursday Saint Athanasius
Acts 15:7-21 **Ps** 96:1-3,10 **Jn** 15:9-11

may

1 2 3 4 **5** 6 7 8 9 10 11 **12** 13 14 15

You shall love the Lord your God with all your heart, and with all your soul, and with all your mind.

—Matthew 22:37

3 Friday Saints Philip and James

1 Cor 15:1-8 **Ps** 19:2-5 **Jn** 14:6-14

4 Saturday

Acts 16:1-10 **Ps** 100:1-3,5 **Jn** 15:18-21

16 17 18 **19** 20 21 22 23 24 25 **26** 27 28 29 30 31

If you love me, you will keep my commandments.

—John 14:15

5 Sunday

Acts 8:5-8,14-17 Ps 66:1-7,16,20 1 Pt 3:15-18 Jn 14:15-21

_____

_____

_____

_____

_____

_____

_____

_____

_____

_____

6 Monday

Acts 16:11-15 Ps 149:1-6,9 Jn 15:26–16:4a

_____

_____

_____

_____

_____

_____

_____

_____

_____

_____

_____

may

1 2 3 4 **5** 6 7 8 9 10 11 **12** 13 14 15

God is rich to all who call upon him, for he can give them nothing better than himself.

—St. Bernard of Clairvaux

7 Tuesday

Acts 16:22-34 **Ps** 138:1-3,7-8 **Jn** 16:5-11

8 Wednesday

Acts 17:15,22–18:1 **Ps** 148:1-2,11-14 **Jn** 16:12-15

16 17 18 **19** 20 21 22 23 24 25 **26** 27 28 29 30 31

May the God of hope fill you with all joy and peace in believing,
so that by the power of the Holy Spirit you may abound in hope.

—Romans 15:13

9 Thursday Ascension of the Lord

Acts 1:1-11 **Ps** 47:2-3,6-9 **Eph** 1:17-23 **Mt** 28:16-20

Holy Day of Obligation

10 Friday Blessed Damien Joseph de Veuster of Moloka'i

Acts 18:9-18 **Ps** 47:2-7 **Jn** 16:20-23a

may

1 2 3 4 **5** 6 7 8 9 10 11 **12** 13 14 15

Let your manner of life be worthy of the gospel of Christ.

—Philippians 1:27

Saturday 11

Acts 18:23-28 **Ps** 47:2-3,8-10 **Jn** 16:23b-28

_____
_____
_____
_____
_____
_____
_____
_____
_____
_____
_____
_____

Sunday 12

Acts 1:12-14 **Ps** 27:1,4,7-8 **1 Pt** 4:13-16 **Jn** 17:1-11a

_____
_____
_____
_____
_____
_____
_____
_____
_____
_____
_____
_____

16 17 18 **19** 20 21 22 23 24 25 **26** 27 28 29 30 31

We ought to respect the image of God in everyone. It is there.

—Blessed Raphaela Mary

13 Monday

Acts 19:1-8 **Ps** 68:2-7 **Jn** 16:29-33

14 Tuesday Saint Matthias

Acts 1:15-17,20-26 **Ps** 113:1-8 **Jn** 15:9-17

may

1 2 3 4 **5** 6 7 8 9 10 11 **12** 13 14 15

As you received Christ Jesus the Lord, so live in him, rooted and built up in him and established in faith.

—Colossians 2:6-7

15 Wednesday Saint Isidore the Farmer

Acts 20:28-38 Ps 68:29-30,33-36 Jn 17:11b-19

16 ~~Thursday~~ Sunday

Acts 22:30; 23:6-11 Ps 16:1-2,5,7-11 Jn 17:20-26

Margaret went to hospital —
Eleanor said she was admitted but
not in room yet

Went to Mass at North ?
Shopped at A & P —

16 17 18 **19** 20 21 22 23 24 25 **26** 27 28 29 30 31

He does much in the sight of God who does his best, be it ever
so little.

—St. Peter of Alcantara

17 ~~Friday~~ Monday

Acts 25:13b-21 **Ps** 103:1-2,11-12,19-20 **Jn** 21:15-19

Tried to get Mommi — no answer

18 Saturday Saint John I

Acts 28:16-20,30-31 **Ps** 11:4-5,7 **Jn** 21:20-25

may

1 2 3 4 **5** 6 7 8 9 10 11 **12** 13 14 15

They were all filled with the Holy Spirit and began to speak in other tongues, as the Spirit gave them utterance.

—Acts 2:4

19 Pentecost Sunday

Acts 2:1-11 **Ps** 104:1,24,29-31,34 **1 Cor** 12:3b-7,12-13 **Jn** 20:19-23

20 Monday Saint Bernardine of Siena

Jas 3:13-18 **Ps** 19:8-10,15 **Mk** 9:14-29

16 17 18 **19** 20 21 22 23 24 25 **26** 27 28 29 30 31

Draw near to God and he will draw near to you.

21 Tuesday
Jas 4:1-10 **Ps** 55:7-11,23 **Mk** 9:30-37

22 Wednesday
Jas 4:13-17 **Ps** 49:2-3,6-11 **Mk** 9:38-40

may

1 2 3 4 **5** 6 7 8 9 10 11 **12** 13 14 15

In the royal galley of Divine Love, there is no galley slave: all the rowers are volunteers.

—St. Francis de Sales

23 Thursday

Jas 5:1-6 **Ps** 49:14-20 **Mk** 9:41-50

24 Friday

Jas 5:9-12 **Ps** 103:1-4,8-9,11-12 **Mk** 10:1-12

16 17 18 **19** 20 21 22 23 24 25 **26** 27 28 29 30 31

He alone loves the Creator perfectly who manifests a pure love for his neighbor.

—St. Bede

25 Saturday Saint Bede the Venerable; Saint Gregory VII;
Saint Mary Magdalene of Pazzi

Jas 5:13-20 **Ps** 141:1-3,8 **Mk** 10:13-16

26 Sunday The Holy Trinity

Ex 34:4b-6, 8-9 (**Ps**) **Dn** 3:52-56 **2 Cor** 13:11-13 **Jn** 3:16-18

may

1 2 3 4 **5** 6 7 8 9 10 11 **12** 13 14 15

Above all hold unfailing your love for one another, since love covers a multitude of sins.

—1 Peter 4:8

27 Monday Saint Augustine of Canterbury

1 Pt 1:3-9 **Ps** 111:1-2,5-6,9-10 **Mk** 10:17-27

_____
_____
_____
_____
_____
_____
_____
_____
_____
_____
_____
_____

28 Tuesday

1 Pt 1:10-16 **Ps** 98:1-4 **Mk** 10:28-31

_____
_____
_____
_____
_____
_____
_____
_____
_____
_____
_____
_____

16 17 18 **19** 20 21 22 23 24 25 **26** 27 28 29 30 31

The Son of man came not to be served but to serve, and to give his life as a ransom for many.

—Mark 10:45

29 Wednesday

1 Pt 1:18-25 Ps 147:12-15,19-20 Mk 10:32-45

30 Thursday

1 Pt 2:2-5,9-12 Ps 100:2-5 Mk 10:46-52

may

1 2 3 4 **5** 6 7 8 9 10 11 **12** 13 14 15

Let the soul of Mary be in each of us to magnify the Lord, and the spirit of Mary be in each of us to rejoice in God.

—St. Anselm

31 Friday The Visitation of the Blessed Virgin Mary

Zep 3:14-18 or **Rom** 12:9-16b (**Ps**) **Is** 12:2-6 **Lk** 1:39-56

This is his commandment, that we should believe in the name of
his Son Jesus Christ and love one another.

—1 John 3:23

may

1 2 3 4 **5** 6 7 8 9 10 11 **12** 13 14 15

The prayer of a righteous man has great power in its effects.

—James 5:16

_____

_____

_____

_____

_____

_____

_____

_____

_____

_____

_____

_____

_____

_____

_____

_____

_____

_____

_____

_____

_____

_____

_____

_____

_____

_____

16 17 18 **19** 20 21 22 23 24 25 **26** 27 28 29 30 31

1 **Saturday** Saint Justin

Jude 17,20b–25 **Ps** 63:2–6 **Mk** 11:27–33

2 **Sunday** The Body and Blood of Christ

Dt 8:2–3,14b–16a **Ps** 147:12–15,19–20 **1 Cor** 10:16–17

Jn 6:51–58

**The Lord is faithful; he will strengthen you and guard
you from evil.** —2 Thessalonians 3:3

May   Forgiveness   9:30 Talk

Monday Saint Charles Lwanga and his companions

2 Pt 1:2-7 **Ps** 91:1-2,14-16 **Mk** 12:1-12

Father forgive them

There was much pain at the time
Jesus had to hand the pain over to
the Father — It was so great a pain —

1762 Father David 22 yrs old ordained
Sulpician

Meets Rose White in Maryland
He sent her to be Educator
1809 Community is started

Father Dubourg, first leader
of Community
Father David appointed 2nd leader

Tuesday

2 Pt 3:12-15a,17-18 **Ps** 90:2-4,10,14,16 **Mk** 12:13-17

He goes to Kentucky at the call
of Father Floyd to start
a new community
1793 Catherine Spalding in Maryland
1812 David gets girls together
Age 19 she is selected Mother
for 6 years — grave poverty

1814 Vows
Ellen O'Connell Deputy teacher
& Teacher Trainer
1831 Angela Spinx — Mother
leaves school to Ellen

16 17 18 19 20 21 22 **23** 24 25 26 27 28 29 **30**

What we ourselves cannot bear let us bear with the help of Christ.
For he tells us: My yoke is easy and my burden is light.

—St. Boniface

Wednesday Saint Boniface

5

2 Tm 1:1-3,6-12 **Ps** 123:1-2 **Mk** 12:18-27

David sees her as a pernicious influence
& takes Ellen from the school &
seems to believe she should not
be in the community

When Ellen sent out to — Arthur
goes also

Factions develop in the
Community of those for & against David

David resigns as Confessor
1833 David resigns completely
& goes to Bardstown
1833 11 Sisters leave the Community
1838 Catherine reelected

Thursday Saint Norbert

6

2 Tm 2:8-15 **Ps** 25:4-5,8-10,14 **Mk** 12:28-34

Her first act is to go to David
in Bardstown
She wants to forgive him
She proceeds to take him home
to Nazareth
"Oh, thank God I have come
back to die among my Sisters"

Eliz & Rose regain their relationship

june

1 2 3 4 5 6 7 8 9 10 11 12 13 14 15

The man who burns with the fire of divine love is a son of the Immaculate Heart of Mary, and wherever he goes, he enkindles that flame. —St. Anthony Mary Claret

7 Friday The Sacred Heart of Jesus

Dt 7:6-11 **Ps** 103:1-4,6-8,10 **1 Jn** 4:7-16 **Mt** 11:25-30

8 Saturday The Immaculate Heart of Mary

2 Tm 4:1-8 **Ps** 71:8-9,14-17,22 **Lk** 2:41-51

16 17 18 19 20 21 22 **23** 24 25 26 27 28 29 **30**

Put on love, which binds everything together in perfect harmony.
—Colossians 3:14

9 Sunday

Hos 6:3-6 **Ps** 50:1,8,12-15 **Rom** 4:18-25 **Mt** 9:9-13

10 Monday

1 Kgs 17:1-6 **Ps** 121:1-8 **Mt** 5:1-12

june

1 2 3 4 5 6 7 8 **9** 10 11 12 13 14 15

Do not be weary in well-doing.

—2 Thessalonians 3:13

11 Tuesday Saint Barnabas

Acts 11:21b–26; 13:1–3   **Ps** 98:1–6   **Mt** 5:13–16

12 Wednesday

1 Kgs 18:20–39   **Ps** 16:1–2,4–5,8,11   **Mt** 5:17–19

16 17 18 19 20 21 22 **23** 24 25 26 27 28 29 **30**

Nothing apart from God can satisfy the human heart which is truly in search of him.

—St. Anthony of Padua

13 Thursday Saint Anthony of Padua

1 Kgs 18:41-46 **Ps** 65:10-13 **Mt** 5:20-26

14 Friday

1 Kgs 19:9a,11-16 **Ps** 27:7-9,13-14 **Mt** 5:27-32

june

1 2 3 4 5 6 7 8 9 10 11 12 13 14 15

Let us hold fast the confession of our hope without wavering, for he who promised is faithful.

—Hebrews 10:23

15 Saturday

1 Kgs 19:19-21 **Ps** 16:1-2,5,7-10 **Mt** 5:33-37

16 Sunday

Ex 19:2-6a **Ps** 100:1-3,5 **Rom** 5:6-11 **Mt** 9:36–10:8

16 17 18 19 20 21 22 **23** 24 25 26 27 28 29 **30**

In this the love of God was made manifest among us, that God sent his only Son into the world, so that we might live through him.

—1 John 4:9

Monday
17

1 Kgs 21:1-16 **Ps** 5:2-3,5-7 **Mt** 5:38-42

Tuesday
18

1 Kgs 21:17-29 **Ps** 51:3-6,11,16 **Mt** 5:43-48

june

1 **2** 3 4 5 6 7 8 **9** 10 11 12 13 14 15

Let every man be quick to hear, slow to speak, slow to anger, for the anger of man does not work the righteousness of God.

—James 1:19-20

19 Wednesday Saint Romuald

2 Kgs 2:1,6-14 **Ps** 31:20-21,24 **Mt** 6:1-6,16-18

20 Thursday

Sir 48:1-14 **Ps** 97:1-7 **Mt** 6:7-15

16 17 18 19 20 21 22 **23** 24 25 26 27 28 29 **30**

Take care above all things not to insult God's boundless
loving kindness.   —St. Aloysius Gonzaga

21 **Friday** Saint Aloysius Gonzaga

2Kgs 11:1-4,9-18,20 **Ps** 132:11-14,17-18 **Mt** 6:19-23

22 **Saturday** Saint Paulinus of Nola; Saints John Fisher and

Thomas More **2 Chr** 24:17-25 **Ps** 89:4-5,29-34 **Mt** 6:24-34

june

1 **2** 3 4 5 6 7 8 **9** 10 11 12 13 14 15

A man may very well lose his head and yet come to no harm—
yea, I say, to unspeakable good and everlasting happiness.
—St. Thomas More

23 Sunday

Jer 20:10-13 **Ps** 69:8-10,14,17,33-35 **Rom** 5:12-15

Mt 10:26-33

24 Monday The Birth of Saint John the Baptist

Is 49:1-6 **Ps** 139:1-3,13-15 **Acts** 13:22-26 **Lk** 1:57-66, 80

16 17 18 19 20 21 22 **23** 24 25 26 27 28 29 **30**

Ask, and it will be given you; seek, and you will find; knock, and it will be opened to you.

—Luke 11:9

25 Tuesday

2 Kgs 19:9b-11,14-21,31-36 **Ps** 48:2-4,10-11 **Mt** 7:6,12-14

26 Wednesday

2 Kgs 22:8-13; 23:1-3 **Ps** 119:33-37,40 **Mt** 7:15-20

june

1　2　3　4　5　6　7　8　**9**　10　11　12　13　14　15

All of us who have received the Holy Spirit are in a sense blended together with one another and with God.

—St. Cyril of Alexandria

27 Thursday Saint Cyril of Alexandria

2 Kgs 24:8-17 **Ps** 79:1-5,8-9 **Mt** 7:21-29

28 Friday Saint Irenaeus

2 Kgs 25:1-12 **Ps** 137:1-6 **Mt** 8:1-4

16 17 18 19 20 21 22 **23** 24 25 26 27 28 29 **30**

Let him who is thirsty come, let him who desires take the water of life without price.

—Revelation 22:17

29 Saturday Saints Peter and Paul

Acts 12:1-11 **Ps** 34:2-9 **2 Tm** 4:6-8,17-18 **Mt** 16:13-19

_____

_____

_____

_____

_____

_____

_____

_____

_____

_____

30 Sunday

2 Kgs 4:8-11,14-16a **Ps** 89:2-3,16-19 **Rom** 6:3-4,8-11

Mt 10:37-42

_____

_____

_____

_____

_____

_____

_____

_____

_____

june

1 **2** 3 4 5 6 7 8 **9** 10 11 12 13 14 15

Surrender yourself completely to the care and the everlasting love
God has for you.

—St. Jane de Chantal

Lord, I am not worthy to have you come under my roof; but only say the word, and my sevant will be healed.

—Matthew 8:8

1 Monday Blessed Junípero Serra

Am 2:6-10,13-16 **Ps** 50:16-23 **Mt** 8:18-22

2 Tuesday

Am 3:1-8; 4:11-12 **Ps** 5:4-8 **Mt** 8:23-27

july

1 2 3 4 5 6 **7** 8 9 10 11 12 13 **14** 15

The true believer practices what he believes.
—St. Gregory the Great

Wednesday Saint Thomas
3
Eph 2:19-22 Ps 117:1-2 Jn 20:24-29

_____

_____

_____

_____

_____

_____

_____

_____

_____

_____

Thursday Saint Elizabeth of Portugal
4
Am 7:10-17 Ps 19:8-11 Mt 9:1-8

_____

_____

_____

_____

_____

_____

_____

_____

_____

_____

16 17 18 19 20 **21** 22 23 24 25 26 27 **28** 29 30 31

A thousand deaths rather than commit one sin!

—St. Maria Goretti

Friday Saint Anthony Mary Zaccaria

5

Am 8:4-6,9-12 **Ps** 119:2,10,20,30,40,131 **Mt** 9:9-13

Saturday Saint Maria Goretti

6

Am 9:11-15 **Ps** 85:9,11-14 **Mt** 9:14-17

july

1 2 3 4 5 6 **7** 8 9 10 11 12 13 **14** 15

Come to me, all who labor and are heavy laden, and I will give you rest.
—Matthew 11:28

7 Sunday

Zec 9:9-10 **Ps** 145:1-2,8-11,13-14 **Rom** 8:9,11-13

Mt 11:25-30

8 Monday

Hos 2:16,17b-18,21-22 **Ps** 145:2-9 **Mt** 9:18-26

16 17 18 19 20 **21** 22 23 24 25 26 27 **28** 29 30 31

In him we live and move and have our being.

9 Tuesday

Hos 8:4-7,11-13 **Ps** 115:3-10 **Mt** 9:32-38

10 Wednesday

Hos 10:1-3,7-8,12 **Ps** 105:2-7 **Mt** 10:1-7

july

1 2 3 4 5 6 **7** 8 9 10 11 12 13 **14** 15

Whenever you begin any good work you should first of all make a pressing appeal to Christ our Lord to bring it to perfection.
—Rule of St. Benedict

11 Thursday Saint Benedict

Hos 11:1-4,8c-9 **Ps** 80:2-3,15-16 **Mt** 10:7-15

_____
_____
_____
_____
_____
_____
_____
_____
_____
_____
_____

12 Friday

Hos 14:2-10 **Ps** 51:3-4,8-9,12-14,17 **Mt** 10:16-23

_____
_____
_____
_____
_____
_____
_____
_____
_____
_____
_____

16 17 18 19 20 **21** 22 23 24 25 26 27 **28** 29 30 31

The sufferings of this present time are not worth comparing with the glory that is to be revealed to us.

—Romans 8:18

13 Saturday Saint Henry

Is 6:1-8 **Ps** 93:1-2,5 **Mt** 10:24-33

14 Sunday

Is 55:10-11 **Ps** 65:10-14 **Rom** 8:18-23 **Mt** 13:1-23

july

1 2 3 4 5 6 **7** 8 9 10 11 12 13 **14** 15

The gate of heaven will be open to all who confide in the protection of Mary.

—St. Bonaventure

15 Monday Saint Bonaventure

Is 1:10-17 **Ps** 50:8-9,16-17,21,23 **Mt** 10:34–11:1

_____

_____

_____

_____

_____

_____

_____

_____

_____

_____

_____

_____

_____

16 Tuesday Our Lady of Mount Carmel

Is 7:1-9 **Ps** 48:2-8 **Mt** 11:20-24

_____

_____

_____

_____

_____

_____

_____

_____

_____

_____

_____

_____

16 17 18 19 20 **21** 22 23 24 25 26 27 **28** 29 30 31

I can do all things in him who strengthens me.

—Philippians 4:13

17 Wednesday

Is 10:5-7,13-16 **Ps** 94:5-10,14-15 **Mt** 11:25-27

18 Thursday Saint Camillus de Lellis

Is 26:7-9,12,16-19 **Ps** 102:13-21 **Mt** 11:28-30

july

1 2 3 4 5 6 **7** 8 9 10 11 12 13 **14** 15

Jesus calls us by our name and the tone of his voice is unmistakable.

—Blessed Josemariá Escrivá

21 Sunday

Wis 12:13,16–19 **Ps** 86:5-6,9-10,15-16 **Rom** 8:26–27

Mt 13:24–43

22 Monday Saint Mary Magdalene

Mi 6:1-4,6-8 **Ps** 63:2-6,8-9 **Jn** 20:1-2, 11-18

july

1 2 3 4 5 6 **7** 8 9 10 11 12 13 **14** 15

Whoever does the will of my Father in heaven is my brother, and sister, and mother.

—Matthew 12:50

23 Tuesday Saint Bridget of Sweden

Mi 7:14-15,18-20 **Ps** 85:2-8 **Mt** 12:46-50

24 Wednesday

Jer 1:1,4-10 **Ps** 71:1-6,15,17 **Mt** 13:1-9

16 17 18 19 20 **21** 22 23 24 25 26 27 **28** 29 30 31

See what love the Father has given us, that we should be called children of God; and so we are.

—1 John 3:1

25 Thursday Saint James

2 Cor 4:7-15 **Ps** 126:1-6 **Mt** 20:20-28

_____
_____
_____
_____
_____
_____
_____
_____
_____
_____
_____

26 Friday Saints Joachim and Anne

Jer 3:14-17 **(Ps) Jer** 31:10-13 **Mt** 13:18-23

_____
_____
_____
_____
_____
_____
_____
_____
_____
_____

july

1 2 3 4 5 6 **7** 8 9 10 11 12 13 **14** 15

In everything God works for good with those who love him, who are called according to his purpose.
—Romans 8:28

27 Saturday

Jer 7:1-11 **Ps** 84:3-6,8,11 **Mt** 13:24-30

28 Sunday

1 Kgs 3:5,7-12 **Ps** 119:57,72,76-77,127-130 **Rom** 8:28-30
Mt 13:44-52

16 17 18 19 20 **21** 22 23 24 25 26 27 **28** 29 30 31

The poor stretches forth the hand, but God receives what is
offered.   —St. Peter Chrysologus

29 Monday Saint Martha

Jer 13:1-11 (**Ps**) **Dt** 32:18-21 **Jn** 11:19-27 or **Lk** 10:38-42

30 Tuesday Saint Peter Chrysologus

Jer 14:17-22 **Ps** 79:8-9,11,13 **Mt** 13:36-43

july

1 2 3 4 5 6 **7** 8 9 10 11 12 13 **14** 15

Your first and greatest asset will be a distrust of self together with a great and magnanimous trust in God.

—St. Ignatius of Loyola

31

Wednesday Saint Ignatius of Loyola

Jer 15:10,16–21 **Ps** 59:2–4,10–11,17–18 **Mt** 13:44–46

16 17 18 19 20 **21** 22 23 24 25 26 27 **28** 29 30 31

Love is patient and kind; love is not jealous or boastful; it is not arrogant or rude. Love does not insist on its own way.

—1 Corinthians 13:4-5

july

1 2 3 4 5 6 **7** 8 9 10 11 12 13 **14** 15

I pray God may open your eyes and let you see what hidden treasures he bestows on us in the trials from which the world thinks only to flee.
—St. John of Avila

16 17 18 19 20 **21** 22 23 24 25 26 27 **28** 29 30 31

> When did it ever happen that a man had confidence in God and
> was lost?　　　　　　　　　　　　　—St. Alphonsus Liguori

1 **Thursday** Saint Alphonsus Liguori

Jer 18:1-6　**Ps** 146:1-6　**Mt** 13:47-53

2 **Friday** Saint Eusebius of Vercelli

Jer 26:1-9　**Ps** 69:6,8-10,14　**Mt** 13:54-58

august

1　2　3　**4**　5　6　7　8　9　10　**11**　12　13　14　15

Never pass a day without thanking Jesus Christ for all he has done
for you during your life. —St. John Vianney

Saturday
3

Jer 26:11-16,24 **Ps** 69:15-16,30-31,33-34 **Mt** 14:1-12

_____

_____

_____

_____

_____

_____

_____

_____

_____

_____

_____

Sunday
4

Is 55:1-3 **Ps** 145:8-9,15-18 **Rom** 8:35,37-39 **Mt** 14:13-21

_____

_____

_____

_____

_____

_____

_____

_____

_____

_____

_____

When Christ appears we will be like him, for we shall
see him as he is.

—1 John 3:2

5 **Monday** Dedication of the Basilica of Saint Mary in Rome

Jer 28:1-17 **Ps** 119:29,43,79-80,95,102 **Mt** 14:22-36

---

6 **Tuesday** Transfiguration of the Lord

Dn 7:9-10,13-14 **Ps** 97:1-2,5-6,9 **2 Pt** 1:16-19 **Mt** 17:1-9

---

august

1 2 3 4 5 6 7 8 9 10 **11** 12 13 14 15

The light shines in the darkness, and the darkness has not overcome it. —John 1:5

7 Wednesday Saint Sixtus II; Saint Cajetan
Jer 31:1-7 (**Ps**) **Jer** 31:10-13 **Mt** 15:21-28

---

8 Thursday Saint Dominic
Jer 31:31-34 **Ps** 51:12-15,18-19 **Mt** 16:13-23

---

16 17 **18** 19 20 21 22 23 24 **25** 26 27 28 29 30 31

Heaven is filled with converted sinners of all kinds and there is room for more. —St. Joseph Cafasso

9 Friday

Na 2:1,3; 3:1–3,6–7 **(Ps) Dt** 32:35–36,39,41 **Mt** 16:24–28

10 Saturday Saint Lawrence

2 Cor 9:6–10 **Ps** 112:1–2,5–9 **Jn** 12:24–26

august

1 2 3 4 5 6 7 8 9 10 **11** 12 13 14 15

Do you not know that you are God's temple and that God's Spirit dwells in you? —1 Corinthians 3:16

11 Sunday

1 Kgs 19:9a,11-13a   Ps 85:9-14   Rom 9:1-5   Mt 14:22-33

12 Monday

Ez 1:2-5,24-28c   Ps 148:1-2,11-14   Mt 17:22-27

16 17 **18** 19 20 21 22 23 24 **25** 26 27 28 29 30 31

God is worthy of glory beyond measure, and therefore it is of supreme importance to seek that glory with all the power of our feeble resources. —St. Maximilian Kolbe

13 Tuesday Saints Pontian and Hippolytus

Ez 2:8–3:4 **Ps** 119:14,24,72,103,111,131 **Mt** 18:1-5,10,12-14

14 Wednesday Saint Maximilian Mary Kolbe

Ez 9:1-7; 10:18-22 **Ps** 113:1-6 **Mt** 18:15-20

august

1 2 3 4 5 6 7 8 9 10 **11** 12 13 14 15

When death had been conquered, Mary was carried up body and
soul to the glory of heaven   —Pope Pius XII

15 Thursday Assumption of the Blessed Virgin Mary

Rv 11:19a; 12:1-6a,10 **Ps** 45:10-12,16 **1 Cor** 15:20-27 **Lk** 1:39-56

Holy Day of Obligation

16 Friday Saint Stephen of Hungary

Ez 16:1-15,60,63 (**Ps**) **Is** 12:2-6 **Mt** 19:3-12

16 17 **18** 19 20 21 22 23 24 **25** 26 27 28 29 30 31

The accomplishment of the divine will is the sole end for which we are in the world.

—St. John Eudes

17 Saturday

Ez 18:1-10,13b,30-32 Ps 51:12-15,18-19 Mt 19:13-15

18 Sunday

Is 56:1,6-7 Ps 67:2-3,5-6,8 Rom 11:13-15,29-32

Mt 15:21-28

august

1 2 3 4 5 6 7 8 9 10 11 12 13 14 15

My Lord, how good you are to those who seek you! Imagine how
good you will be to those who find you!

—St. Bernard of Clairvaux

19 Monday Saint John Eudes

Ez 24:15-24 (Ps) Dt 32:18-21 Mt 19:16-22

20 Tuesday Saint Bernard

Ez 28:1-10 (Ps) Dt 32:26-28,30,35-36 Mt 19:23-30

16 17 **18** 19 20 21 22 23 24 **25** 26 27 28 29 30 31

Holy Communion is the shortest and safest way to heaven.
—St. Pius X

21 Wednesday Saint Pius X

Ez 34:1-11 **Ps** 23:1-6 **Mt** 20:1-16a

22 Thursday Queenship of the Blessed Virgin Mary

Ez 36:23-28 **Ps** 51:12-15,18-19 **Mt** 22:1-14

august

1 2 3 4 5 6 7 8 9 10 **11** 12 13 14 15

Whatever you do, in word or deed, do everything in the name of the Lord Jesus, giving thanks to God the Father through him.

—Colossians 3:17

23 Friday Saint Rose of Lima

Ez 37:1-14 **Ps** 107:2-9 **Mt** 22:34-40

_____

_____

_____

_____

_____

_____

_____

_____

_____

_____

_____

24 Saturday Saint Bartholomew

Rv 21:9b-14 **Ps** 145:10-13,17-18 **Jn** 1:45-51

_____

_____

_____

_____

_____

_____

_____

_____

_____

_____

_____

16 17 **18** 19 20 21 22 23 24 **25** 26 27 28 29 30 31

O the depth of the riches and wisdom and knowledge of God!
How unsearchable are his judgments and how inscrutable his ways!
—Romans 11:33

25 Sunday

Is 22:19–23 **Ps** 138:2–3,6,8 **Rom** 11:33–36 **Mt** 16:13–20

26 Monday

2 Thes 1:1–5,11b–12 **Ps** 96:1–5 **Mt** 23:13–22

august

1 2 3 **4** 5 6 7 8 9 10 **11** 12 13 14 15

If you desire to praise the Lord, then live what you express. Live good lives, and you yourselves will be his praise.

—St. Augustine

27 Tuesday Saint Monica

2 Thes 2:1–3a,14–17 **Ps** 96:10–13 **Mt** 23:23–26

_____

_____

_____

_____

_____

_____

_____

_____

_____

_____

28 Wednesday Saint Augustine

2 Thes 3:6–10,16–18 **Ps** 128:1–2,4–5 **Mt** 23:27–32

_____

_____

_____

_____

_____

_____

_____

_____

_____

_____

16 17 **18** 19 20 21 22 23 24 **25** 26 27 28 29 30 31

Bear fruit that befits repentance.

29 Thursday Martyrdom of Saint John the Baptist

1 Cor 1:1-9 **Ps** 71:1-6,15,17 **Mk** 6:17-29

30 Friday

1 Cor 1:17-25 **Ps** 33:1-2,4-5,10-11 **Mt** 25:1-13

august

1 2 3 4 5 6 7 8 9 10 **11** 12 13 14 15

> The time we spend in having our daily audience with God is the
> most precious part of the whole day.
>
> —Mother Teresa of Calcutta

31 Saturday

1 Cor 1:26-31 **Ps** 33:12-13,18-21 **Mt** 25:14-30

16 17 **18** 19 20 21 22 23 24 **25** 26 27 28 29 30 31

Watch and pray that you may not enter into temptation; the spirit indeed is willing, but the flesh is weak.

—Mark 14:38

_____

_____

_____

_____

_____

_____

_____

_____

_____

_____

_____

_____

_____

_____

_____

_____

_____

_____

_____

_____

_____

_____

_____

_____

august

1 2 3 4 5 6 7 8 9 10 **11** 12 13 14 15

I think that if God forgives us we must forgive ourselves.
Otherwise it is almost like setting up ourselves as a higher tribunal
than him.   —C. S. Lewis

16 17 **18** 19 20 21 22 23 24 **25** 26 27 28 29 30 31

Do not be conformed to this world but be transformed by the
renewal of your mind.

—Romans 12:2

1 Sunday

Jer 20:7-9 **Ps** 63:2-6,8-9 **Rom** 12:1-2 **Mt** 16:21-27

2 Monday

1 Cor 2:1-5 **Ps** 119:97-102 **Lk** 4:16-30

september

1 2 3 4 5 6 7 **8** 9 10 11 12 13 14 **15**

When one practices first and preaches afterwards, one is really teaching with power.

—St. Gregory the Great

3 Tuesday Saint Gregory the Great

1 Cor 2:10b-16 **Ps** 145:8-14 **Lk** 4:31-37

4 Wednesday

1 Cor 3:1-9 **Ps** 33:12-15,20-21 **Lk** 4:38-44

He is before all things, and in him all things hold together.
—Colossians 1:17

5 Thursday

1 Cor 3:18-23 Ps 24:1-6 Lk 5:1-11

6 Friday

1 Cor 4:1-5 Ps 37:3-6,27-28,39-40 Lk 5:33-39

september

1 2 3 4 5 6 7 **8** 9 10 11 12 13 14 **15**

Prayer is the attention of the soul fixed lovingly on Jesus.
The more loving that attention is, the better is the prayer.
—Charles de Foucauld

Saturday

7

1 Cor 4:6b-15 **Ps** 145:17-21 **Lk** 6:1-5

_____

_____

_____

_____

_____

_____

_____

_____

_____

_____

_____

Sunday

8

Ez 33:7-9 **Ps** 95:1-2,6-9 **Rom** 13:8-10 **Mt** 18:15-20

_____

_____

_____

_____

_____

_____

_____

_____

_____

_____

_____

_____

16 17 18 19 20 21 **22** 23 24 25 26 27 28 **29** 30

To do the will of God man must despise his own: the more he dies to himself, the more he will live to God.

—St. Peter Claver

9 Monday Saint Peter Claver

1 Cor 5:1-8 **Ps** 5:5-7,12 **Lk** 6:6-11

10 Tuesday

1 Cor 6:1-11 **Ps** 149:1-6,9 **Lk** 6:12-19

september

1 2 3 4 5 6 7 **8** 9 10 11 12 13 14 **15**

If a man loves me, he will keep my word, and my Father will love him, and we will come to him and make our home with him.
—John 14:23

11 Wednesday

1 Cor 7:25-31 **Ps** 45:11-12,14-17 **Lk** 6:20-26

_____
_____
_____
_____
_____
_____
_____
_____
_____
_____
_____
_____

12 Thursday

1 Cor 8:1b-7,11-13 **Ps** 139: 1-3,13-14,23-24 **Lk** 6:27-38

_____
_____
_____
_____
_____
_____
_____
_____
_____
_____
_____
_____

16 17 18 19 20 21 **22** 23 24 25 26 27 28 **29** 30

Do you wish to receive mercy? Show mercy to your neighbor.
—St. John Chrysostom

13 Friday Saint John Chrysostom

1 Cor 9:16-19,22b-27 **Ps** 84:3-6,8,12 **Lk** 6:39-42

14 Saturday Exaltation of the Holy Cross

Nm 21:4b-9 **Ps** 78:1-2,34-38 **Phil** 2:6-11 **Jn** 3:13-17

september

1 2 3 4 5 6 7 **8** 9 10 11 12 13 14 **15**

Patient waiting is necessary if we are to be perfected in what we have begun to be, and if we are to receive from God what we hope for and believe. —St. Cyprian

15 Sunday

Sir 27:30–28:9 **Ps** 103:1-4,9-12 **Rom** 14:7-9 **Mt** 18:21-35

16 Monday Saints Cornelius and Cyprian

1 Cor 11:17-26,33 **Ps** 40:7-10,17 **Lk** 7:1-10

16 17 18 19 20 21 **22** 23 24 25 26 27 28 **29** 30

You have been created for the glory of God and your eternal salvation. This is your goal; this is the treasure of your heart.
—St. Robert Bellarmine

17 Tuesday Saint Robert Bellarmine

1 Cor 12:12-14,27-31a Ps 100:1-5 Lk 7:11-17

18 Wednesday

1 Cor 12:31–13:13 Ps 33:2-5,12,22 Lk 7:31-35

september

1 2 3 4 5 6 7 **8** 9 10 11 12 13 14 **15**

God loves a cheerful giver.

19 Thursday Saint Januarius

1 Cor 15:1-11 **Ps** 118:1-2,16-17,28 **Lk** 7:36-50

_____

_____

_____

_____

_____

_____

_____

_____

_____

_____

_____

_____

20 Friday Saints Andrew Kim and Paul Hasang

1 Cor 15:12-20 **Ps** 17:1,6-8,15 **Lk** 8:1-3

_____

_____

_____

_____

_____

_____

_____

_____

_____

_____

_____

_____

16 17 18 19 20 21 **22** 23 24 25 26 27 28 **29** 30

I came not to call the righteous but sinners.

—Matthew 9:13

21 Saturday Saint Matthew
Eph 4:1-7,11-13 **Ps** 19:2-5 **Mt** 9:9-13

22 Sunday
Is 55:6-9 **Ps** 145:2-3,8-9,17-18 **Phil** 1:20c-24,27a **Mt** 20:1-16a

september

1 2 3 4 5 6 7 **8** 9 10 11 12 13 14 **15**

You must live each day as it comes, and proceed arm in arm with Providence, not try to race ahead.

—Pope John XXIII

23 Monday

Prv 3:27-34 **Ps** 15:2-5 **Lk** 8:16-18

24 Tuesday

Prv 21:1-6,10-13 **Ps** 119:1,27,30,34-35,44 **Lk** 8:19-21

16 17 18 19 20 21 **22** 23 24 25 26 27 28 **29** 30

Be steadfast, immovable, always abounding in the work of the Lord, knowing that in the Lord your labor is not in vain.

—1 Corinthians 15:58

25 Wednesday

Prv 30:5-9 **Ps** 119:29,72,89,101,104,163 **Lk** 9:1-6

26 Thursday Saints Cosmas and Damian

Eccl 1:2-11 **Ps** 90:3-6,12-14,17 **Lk** 9:7-9

september

1 2 3 4 5 6 7 **8** 9 10 11 12 13 14 **15**

> God loves the poor, and consequently he loves those who have an affection for the poor.
>
> —St. Vincent de Paul

27 Friday Saint Vincent de Paul

Eccl 3:1-11 Ps 144:1-4 Lk 9:18-22

28 Saturday Saint Wenceslaus; Saint Lawrence Ruiz and his companions

Eccl 11:9–12:8 Ps 90:3-6,12-14,17 Lk 9:43b-45

It is ours to offer what we can, his to supply what we cannot.
—St. Jerome

29 Sunday

Ez 18:25-28 **Ps** 25:4-9 **Phil** 2:1-11 **Mt** 21:28-32

_____

_____

_____

_____

_____

_____

_____

_____

_____

_____

30 Monday Saint Jerome

Jb 1:6-22 **Ps** 17:1-3,6-7 **Lk** 9:46-50

_____

_____

_____

_____

_____

_____

_____

_____

_____

_____

september

1 2 3 4 5 6 7 **8** 9 10 11 12 13 14 **15**

My soul magnifies the Lord, and my spirit rejoices in
God my Savior.

—Luke 1:46-47

_____

_____

_____

_____

_____

_____

_____

_____

_____

_____

_____

_____

_____

A Reminder

All of us at *The Word Among Us* hope that this
year's "Discipleship" theme has been
inspirational for your prayer and journaling. Since
so many people begin selecting calendars and
planners at this time, we want to encourage you to
reserve your copy of next year's edition now. If you
find that *The Word Among Us* Prayer Journal has added to your
prayer and appreciation of scripture, please make it a point to call
toll free this week:

1-800-775-9673.

or order online at www.wau.org

Visa, MasterCard, Discover Card accepted.

May you find the holidays ahead a time of blessing, and may the
Lord see you into a new year full of joy.

Without love all we do is worthless.

—St. Thérèse of Lisieux

1 Tuesday Saint Thérèse of Lisieux

Jb 3:1-3,11-17,20-23 **Ps** 88:2-8 **Lk** 9:51-56

2 Wednesday Guardian Angels

Jb 9:1-12,14-16 **Ps** 91:1-6,10-11 **Mt** 18:1-5,10

October

1 2 3 4 5 **6** 7 8 9 10 11 12 **13** 14 15

Spiritual joy arises from purity of the heart and perseverance in prayer. —St. Francis of Assisi

3 Thursday

Jb 19:21-27 **Ps** 27:7-9,13-14 **Lk** 10:1-12

4 Friday Saint Francis of Assisi

Jb 38:1,12-21; 40:3-5 **Ps** 139:1-3,7-10,13-14 **Lk** 10:13-16

16 17 18 19 **20** 21 22 23 24 25 26 **27** 28 29 30 31

> Have no anxiety about anything, but in everything by prayer and supplication with thanksgiving let your requests be made known to God.
> —Philippians 4:6

5 Saturday

Jb 42:1-3,5-6,12-17 **Ps** 119:66,71,75,91,125,130 **Lk** 10:17-24

6 Sunday

Is 5:1-7 **Ps** 80:9,12-16,19-20 **Phil** 4:6-9 **Mt** 21:33-43

october

1 2 3 4 5 **6** 7 8 9 10 11 12 **13** 14 15

The Holy Rosary is the storehouse of countless blessings.

—Blessed Alan de la Roche

7 Monday Our Lady of the Rosary
Gal 1:6-12 Ps 111:1-2,7-10 Lk 10:25-37

8 Tuesday
Gal 1:13-24 Ps 139:1-3,13-15 Lk 10:38-42

16 17 18 19 **20** 21 22 23 24 25 26 **27** 28 29 30 31

Forgive, if you have anything against any one; so that your Father also who is in heaven may forgive you your trespasses. —Mark 11:25

9 Wednesday Saint Denis and his companions; Saint John Leonardi

Gal 2:1-2,7-14 **Ps** 117:1-2 **Lk** 11:1-4

10 Thursday

Gal 3:1-5 **(Ps) Lk** 1:69-75 **Lk** 11:5-13

october

1 2 3 4 5 **6** 7 8 9 10 11 12 **13** 14 15

Trust the past to the mercy of God, the present to his love, and the future to his providence.

—St. Augustine

11 Friday

Gal 3:7-14 **Ps** 111:1-6 **Lk** 11:15-26

12 Saturday

Gal 3:22-29 **Ps** 105:2-7 **Lk** 11:27-28

16 17 18 19 **20** 21 22 23 24 25 26 **27** 28 29 30 31

Let each of you look not only to his own interests, but to the
interests of others.

—Philippians 2:4

13 Sunday
Is 25:6-10a Ps 23:1-6 Phil 4:12-14,19-20 Mt 22:1-14

14 Monday Saint Callistus I
Gal 4:22-24,26-27,31–5:1 Ps 113:1-7 Lk 11:29-32

October

1 2 3 4 5 **6** 7 8 9 10 11 12 **13** 14 15

We will never reach perfection in the love of neighbor if that love does not rise from love of God as its root.

—St. Teresa of Avila

15 Tuesday Saint Teresa of Avila

Gal 5:1-6 **Ps** 119:41,43-45,47-48 **Lk** 11:37-41

16 Wednesday Saint Hedwig; Saint Margaret Mary Alacoque

Gal 5:18-25 **Ps** 1:1-4,6 **Lk** 11:42-46

16 17 18 19 **20** 21 22 23 24 25 26 **27** 28 29 30 31

There is one physician, fleshly and spiritual, begotten and unbegotten, God in man, true life in death . . . Jesus Christ our Lord.
—St. Ignatius of Antioch

17 Thursday Saint Ignatius of Antioch

Eph 1:1-10 **Ps** 98:1-6 **Lk** 11:47-54

18 Friday Saint Luke

2 Tm 4:10-17b **Ps** 145:10-13,17-18 **Lk** 10:1-9

october

1 2 3 4 5 **6** 7 8 9 10 11 12 **13** 14 15

Jesus, my Lord and Savior, what can I give you in return for all the favors you have first conferred on me?

—St. John de Brébeuf

19 Saturday Saints Isaac Jogues and John de Brébeuf and their companions Eph 1:15-23 Ps 8:2-7 Lk 12:8-12

_____

_____

_____

_____

_____

_____

_____

_____

_____

_____

_____

_____

20 Sunday
Is 45:1,4-6 Ps 96:1,3-5,7-10 1 Thes 1:1-5b Mt 22:15-21

_____

_____

_____

_____

_____

_____

_____

_____

_____

_____

_____

16 17 18 19 **20** 21 22 23 24 25 26 **27** 28 29 30 31

Watch therefore, for you do not know on what day your Lord is coming.
—Matthew 24:42

21 Monday
Eph 2:1-10 **Ps** 100:2-5 **Lk** 12:13-21

22 Tuesday
Eph 2:12-22 **Ps** 85:9-14 **Lk** 12:35-38

october

1 2 3 4 5 **6** 7 8 9 10 11 12 **13** 14 15

Our Lord has created persons for all states of life, and in all of them we see people who have achieved sanctity by fulfilling their obligations well. —St. Anthony Mary Claret

23 Wednesday

Eph 3:2-12 (**Ps**) **Is** 12:2-6 **Lk** 12:39-48

24 Thursday Saint Anthony Mary Claret

Eph 3:14-21 **Ps** 33:1-2,4-5,11-12,18-19 **Lk** 12:49-53

16 17 18 19 **20** 21 22 23 24 25 26 **27** 28 29 30 31

Love is not irritable or resentful; it does not rejoice at wrong, but rejoices in the right.

—1 Corinthians 13:5-6

25 Friday

Eph 4:1-6 **Ps** 24:1-6 **Lk** 12:54-59

26 Saturday

Eph 4:7-16 **Ps** 122:1-5 **Lk** 13:1-9

october

1 2 3 4 5 **6** 7 8 9 10 11 12 **13** 14 15

Whatever your task, work heartily, as serving the Lord and not men, knowing that from the Lord you will receive the inheritance as your reward. —Colossians 3:23-24

27 Sunday

Ex 22:20-26 Ps 18:2-4,47,51 **1 Thes** 1:5c-10 **Mt** 22:34-40

28 Monday Saints Simon and Jude

Eph 2:19-22 **Ps** 19:2-5 **Lk** 6:12-16

16 17 18 19 **20** 21 22 23 24 25 26 **27** 28 29 30 31

Do not do anything you cannot offer to God.

—St. John Vianney

29 Tuesday
Eph 5:21-33 **Ps** 128:1-5 **Lk** 13:18-21

30 Wednesday
Eph 6:1-9 **Ps** 145:10-14 **Lk** 13:22-30

october

1 2 3 4 5 **6** 7 8 9 10 11 12 **13** 14 15

Little children, let us not love in word or speech but in deed and in truth.

—1 John 3:18

31 Thursday

Eph 6:10-20 **Ps** 144:1-2,9-10 **Lk** 13:31-35

16 17 18 19 **20** 21 22 23 24 25 26 **27** 28 29 30 31

Hallelujah! Salvation and glory and power belong to our God, for his judgments are true and just.

—Revelation 19:1-2

october

1   2   3   4   5   **6**   7   8   9   10   11   12   **13**   14   15

If we say less than we should it is easy to add, but having said too much it is hard to take it off.

—St. Francis de Sales

16 17 18 19 **20** 21 22 23 24 25 26 **27** 28 29 30 31

> You cannot be half a saint. You must be a whole saint or
> no saint at all.
> —St. Thérèse of Lisieux

1 Friday All Saints

Rv 7:2-4,9-14 **Ps** 24:1-6 **1 Jn** 3:1-3 **Mt** 5:1-12a

Holy Day of Obligation

2 Saturday All Souls

Dn 12:1-3 **Ps** 27:1,4,7-9,13-14 **Rom** 6:3-9 **Jn** 6:37-40

november

1 2 **3** 4 5 6 7 8 9 **10** 11 12 13 14 15

We must keep ourselves in the presence of God as much as possible and have no other view or end in all our actions but the divine honor. —St. Charles Borromeo

3 Sunday

Mal 1:14b–2:2b,8-10 **Ps** 131:1-3 **1 Thes** 2:7b-9,13 **Mt** 23:1-12

---

4 Monday Saint Charles Borromeo

Phil 2:1-4 **Ps** 131:1-3 **Lk** 14:12-14

---

16 **17** 18 19 20 21 22 23 **24** 25 26 27 28 29 30

No one who puts his hand to the plow and looks back is fit for the kingdom of God.

—Luke 9:62

5 Tuesday

Phil 2:5-11 **Ps** 22:26-32 **Lk** 14:15-24

6 Wednesday

Phil 2:12-18 **Ps** 27:1,4,13-14 **Lk** 14:25-33

november

1 2 **3** 4 5 6 7 8 9 **10** 11 12 13 14 15

I count everything as loss because of the surpassing worth of knowing Christ Jesus my Lord.

—Philippians 3:8

7 Thursday

Phil 3:3-8a **Ps** 105:2-7 **Lk** 15:1-10

8 Friday

Phil 3:17–4:1 **Ps** 122:1-5 **Lk** 16:1-8

16 **17** 18 19 20 21 22 23 **24** 25 26 27 28 29 30

Never utter in your neighbor's absence what you would not say in their presence.—   St. Mary Magdalene of Pazzi

9

Saturday Dedication of the Lateran Basilica in Rome

Ez 47:1-2, 8-9, 12 **Ps** 84:3-6,8,11 **1 Cor** 3:9c-11,16-17 **Jn** 2:13-22

_____

_____

_____

_____

_____

_____

_____

_____

_____

_____

_____

10

Sunday

Wis 6:12-16 **Ps** 63:2-8 **1 Thes** 4:13-18 **Mt** 25:1-13

_____

_____

_____

_____

_____

_____

_____

_____

_____

_____

november

1 2 **3** 4 5 6 7 8 9 **10** 11 12 13 14 15

Let love be genuine; hate what is evil, hold fast to what is good.
—Romans 12:9

11 Monday Saint Martin of Tours
Ti 1:1-9 **Ps** 24:1-6 **Lk** 17:1-6

12 Tuesday Saint Josaphat
Ti 2:1-8,11-14 **Ps** 37:3-4,18,23,27,29 **Lk** 17:7-10

Give me your grace, most loving Jesus, and I will run after you to the finish line, forever.

—St. Frances Xavier Cabrini

13 Wednesday Saint Frances Xavier Cabrini

Ti 3:1-7 Ps 23:1-6 Lk 17:11-19

_____

_____

_____

_____

_____

_____

_____

_____

_____

_____

_____

_____

14 Thursday

Phlm 7-20 Ps 146:7-10 Lk 17:20-25

_____

_____

_____

_____

_____

_____

_____

_____

_____

_____

_____

november

1 2 **3** 4 5 6 7 8 9 **10** 11 12 13 14 15

Nothing richer can be offered to God than a good will, for the good will is the originator of all good and is the mother of all virtues.

—St. Albert the Great

15 Friday Saint Albert the Great

2 Jn 4-9 **Ps** 119:1-2,10-11,17-18 **Lk** 17:26-37

16 Saturday Saint Margaret of Scotland; Saint Gertrude the Great

3 Jn 5-8 **Ps** 112:1-6 **Lk** 18:1-8

16 **17** 18 19 20 21 22 23 **24** 25 26 27 28 29 30

As the Lord has forgiven you, so you also must forgive.
—Colossians 3:13

17 Sunday
Prv 31:10-13,19-20,30-31 **Ps** 128:1-5 **1 Thes** 5:1-6 **Mt** 25:14-30

_____

_____

_____

_____

_____

_____

_____

_____

_____

_____

18 Monday The Dedication of the Basilicas of the Apostles Peter and Paul in Rome; Saint Rose Philippine Duchesne
Rv 1:1-4; 2:1-5a **Ps** 1:1-4,6 **Lk** 18:35-43

_____

_____

_____

_____

_____

_____

_____

_____

november

1 2 **3** 4 5 6 7 8 9 **10** 11 12 13 14 15

If we confess our sins, he is faithful and just, and will forgive our sins and cleanse us from all unrighteousness.

—1 John 1:9

19 Tuesday

Rv 3:1-6,14-22 **Ps** 15:2-5 **Lk** 19:1-10

20 Wednesday

Rv 4:1-11 **Ps** 150:1-6 **Lk** 19:11-28

16 **17** 18 19 20 21 22 23 **24** 25 26 27 28 29 30

Mary lived in such a way that her life itself is a lesson for everyone.

—St. Ambrose

21 Thursday The Presentation of the Blessed Virgin Mary
Rv 5:1-10 **Ps** 149:1-6,9 **Lk** 19:41-44

22 Friday Saint Cecilia
Rv 10:8-11 **Ps** 119:14,24,72,103,111,131 **Lk** 19:45-48

november

1 2 **3** 4 5 6 7 8 9 **10** 11 12 13 14 15

Cling to the saints, for those who cling to them will be sanctified.

—St. Clement

23 Saturday Saint Clement I

Rv 11:4-12 **Ps** 144:1-2,9-10 **Lk** 20:27-40

24 Sunday Christ the King

Ez 34:11-12,15-17 **Ps** 23:1-3,5-6 **1 Cor** 15:20-26,28 **Mt** 25:31-46

16 **17** 18 19 20 21 22 23 **24** 25 26 27 28 29 30

Great and wonderful are thy deeds, O Lord God the Almighty! Just and true are thy ways, O King of the ages!

—Revelation 15:3

25 Monday

Rv 14:1-3,4b-5 **Ps** 24:1-6 **Lk** 21:1-4

26 Tuesday

Rv 14:14-19 **Ps** 96:10-13 **Lk** 21:5-11

november

1 2 **3** 4 5 6 7 8 9 **10** 11 12 13 14 15

We should not accept in silence the blessings of God, but return thanks for them.

—St. Basil

27 Wednesday

Rv 15:1-4 **Ps** 98:1-3,7-9 **Lk** 21:12-19

28 Thursday Thanksgiving Day (U.S.)

Rv 18:1-2,21-23; 19:1-3,9a **Ps** 100:2-5 **Lk** 21:20-28

16 **17** 18 19 20 21 22 23 **24** 25 26 27 28 29 30

Follow me, and I will make you fishers of men.

—Matthew 4:19

29 Friday

Rv 20:1-4,11–21:2 **Ps** 84:3-6,8 **Lk** 21:29-33

30 Saturday Saint Andrew

Rom 10:9-18 **Ps** 19:2-5 **Mt** 4:18-22

november

1   2   **3**   4   5   6   7   8   9   **10**   11   12   13   14   15

Continue steadfastly in prayer, being watchful in it with
thanksgiving.   —Colossians 4:2

_____

_____

_____

_____

_____

_____

_____

_____

_____

_____

_____

_____

_____

_____

_____

_____

_____

_____

_____

_____

_____

_____

_____

_____

_____

_____

16 **17** 18 19 20 21 22 23 **24** 25 26 27 28 29 30

Advent opens a new chapter every year in that book of salvation which God writes in the church through the story of man.

—Pope John Paul II

1 First Sunday of Advent

Is 63:16b-17,19b; 64:2b-7 **Ps** 80:2-3,15-16,18-19

1 Cor 1:3-9 **Mk** 13:33-37

2 Monday

Is 2:1-5 **Ps** 122:1-9 **Mt** 8:5-11

December

1 2 3 4 5 6 7 **8** 9 10 11 12 13 14 **15**

Providence is the care God takes of all existing things.
—St. John of Damascus

3 **Tuesday** Saint Francis Xavier
Is 11:1-10 Ps 72:1,7-8,12-13,17 Lk 10:21-24

4 **Wednesday** Saint John of Damascus
Is 25:6-10a Ps 23:1-6 Mt 15:29-37

16 17 18 19 20 21 **22** 23 24 25 26 27 28 **29** 30 31

Let us love one another; for love is of God, and he who loves is born of God and knows God.

—1 John 4:7

5 Thursday

Is 26:1-6 **Ps** 118:1,8-9,19-21,25-27 **Mt** 7:21,24-27

_____

_____

_____

_____

_____

_____

_____

_____

_____

_____

_____

6 Friday Saint Nicholas

Is 29:17-24 **Ps** 27:1,4,13-14 **Mt** 9:27-31

_____

_____

_____

_____

_____

_____

_____

_____

_____

_____

_____

December

1 2 3 4 5 6 7 **8** 9 10 11 12 13 14 **15**

We avoid the eyes of men, and in God's presence we commit sin.
We know God to be judge of all, and yet in his sight we sin.
—St. Ambrose

7 Saturday Saint Ambrose

Is 30:19-21,23-26 Ps 147:1-6 Mt 9:35—10:1,6-8

_____

_____

_____

_____

_____

_____

_____

_____

_____

_____

_____

_____

8 Second Sunday of Advent

Is 40:1-5,9-11 Ps 85:9-14 2 Pt 3:8-14 Mk 1:1-8

_____

_____

_____

_____

_____

_____

_____

_____

_____

_____

_____

16 17 18 19 20 21 **22** 23 24 25 26 27 28 **29** 30 31

Without God's Son, nothing could exist; without Mary's Son, nothing could be redeemed.

—St. Anselm

9 Monday Immaculate Conception of the Blessed Virgin Mary

Gn 3:9-15,20 **Ps** 98:1-4 **Eph** 1:3-6,11-12 **Lk** 1:26-38

10 Tuesday

Is 40:1-11 **Ps** 96:1-3,10-13 **Mt** 18:12-14

December

1 2 3 4 5 6 7 **8** 9 10 11 12 13 14 **15**

Do not be frightened or grieve, or let your heart be dismayed.
Am I not here, I who am your Mother? And is not my help a refuge?
—Our Lady to Blessed Juan Diego

11 Wednesday Saint Damasus I

Is 40:25-31 **Ps** 103:1-4,8,10 **Mt** 11:28-30

12 Thursday Our Lady of Guadalupe

Zec 2:14-17 **Ps** 45:11-12,14-17 **Lk** 1:26-38

16 17 18 19 20 21 **22** 23 24 25 26 27 28 **29** 30 31

The soul who has the hope of heaven achieves all that is hoped for.

—St. John of the Cross

13 Friday Saint Lucy

Is 48:17-19 **Ps** 1:1-4,6 **Mt** 11:16-19

14 Saturday Saint John of the Cross

Sir 48:1-4,9-11 **Ps** 80:2-3,15-16,18-19 **Mt** 17:10-13

December

1 2 3 4 5 6 7 **8** 9 10 11 12 13 14 **15**

Steep yourself in the meaning of these Advent days and above all, pay heed to him who is approaching.   —St. Bernard of Clairvaux

15 Third Sunday of Advent

Is 61:1-2a,10-11 **(Ps) Lk** 1:46-50,53-54 **1 Thes** 5:16-24

Jn 1:6-8,19-28

16 Monday

Nm 24:2-7,15-17a **Ps** 25:4-9 **Mt** 21:23-27

16 17 18 19 20 21 **22** 23 24 25 26 27 28 **29** 30 31

I have come as light into the world, that whoever believes in me
may not remain in darkness.

—John 12:46

17 Tuesday

Gn 49:2,8-10 **Ps** 72:3-4,7-8,17 **Mt** 1:1-17

18 Wednesday

Jer 23:5-8 **Ps** 72:1,12-13,18-19 **Mt** 1:18-24

December

1 2 3 4 5 6 7 **8** 9 10 11 12 13 14 **15**

We live our faith when we are open to God's coming, when we persevere in his advent.

—Pope John Paul II

19 Thursday

Jgs 13:2-7,24-25a Ps 71:3-6,16-17 Lk 1:5-25

20 Friday

Is 7:10-14 Ps 24:1-6 Lk 1:26-38

Bethlehem became a link between heaven and earth; God and man met there and looked each other in the face.

—Archbishop Fulton Sheen

21 Saturday Saint Peter Canisius

Sg 2:8-14 **Ps** 33:2-3,11-12,20-21 **Lk** 1:39-45

22 Fourth Sunday of Advent

2 Sm 7:1-5,8b-12,14a,16 **Ps** 89:2-5,27,29 **Rom** 16:25-27
Lk 1:26-38

December

1 2 3 4 5 6 7 **8** 9 10 11 12 13 14 **15**

Christist is born that by his birth he might restore our nature.
—St. Peter Chrysologus

23 Monday Saint John of Kanty

Mal 3:1-4,23-24 **Ps** 25:4-5,8-10,14 **Lk** 1:57-66

_____

_____

_____

_____

_____

_____

_____

_____

_____

_____

_____

24 Tuesday

2 Sm 7:1-5,8b-12,14a,16 **Ps** 89:2-5,27,29 **Lk** 1:67-79

_____

_____

_____

_____

_____

_____

_____

_____

_____

_____

_____

16 17 18 19 20 21 **22** 23 24 25 26 27 28 **29** 30 31

Behold, I bring you good news of a great joy which will come to all the people; for to you is born this day in the city of David a Savior, who is Christ the Lord.

— Luke 2:10-11

25 Wednesday Christmas

Is 52:7-10 **Ps** 98:1-6 **Heb** 1:1-6 **Jn** 1:1-18

Holy Day of Obligation

26 Thursday Saint Stephen

Acts 6:8-10; 7:54-59 **Ps** 31:3-4,6-8,17,21 **Mt** 10:17-22

December

1 2 3 4 5 6 7 8 9 10 11 12 13 14 15

He became one like us to make us like God.

—St. Francis de Sales

27 Friday Saint John

1 Jn 1:1-4 **Ps** 97:1-2,5-6,11-12 **Jn** 20:2-8

28 Saturday Holy Innocents

1 Jn 1:5–2:2 **Ps** 124:2-5,7-8 **Mt** 2:13-18

16 17 18 19 20 21 **22** 23 24 25 26 27 28 **29** 30 31

May the Holy Family, icon and model of every human family, help each individual to walk in the spirit of Nazareth.

—Pope John Paul II

29 Sunday Holy Family of Jesus, Mary and Joseph

Sir 3:2-7; 12-14 **Ps** 128:1-5 **Col** 3:12-21 **Lk** 2:22-40

30 Monday

1 Jn 2:12-17 **Ps** 96:7-10 **Lk** 2:36-40

December

1 2 3 4 5 6 7 **8** 9 10 11 12 13 14 **15**

The Word became flesh and dwelt among us, full of grace and
truth; we have beheld his glory, glory as of the only Son from the
Father.   —John 1:14

31 Tuesday Saint Sylvester I

1 Jn 2:18-21 **Ps** 96:1-2,11-13 **Jn** 1:1-18

He who had his birth in Bethlehem came to be born in the hearts of men. For, what would it profit if he was born a thousand times in Bethlehem unless he was born again in man?

—Angelus Silesius

December

1 2 3 4 5 6 7 **8** 9 10 11 12 13 14 **15**

> Be attentive to God's message and diligently follow the path God
> tells you to take.
> —St. Ambrose

Prayer Notes

Prayer Notes

Reserve Next Year's Prayer Journal Today!

The Word Among Us 2003 Prayer Journal

Continue your journey of faith with next year's *Prayer Journal*. As always, you'll get inspirational quotes, and a complete listing of the daily Mass readings, saints' feast days, and holy days of obligation. Give it as a gift and introduce a friend to the pleasures of journaling.

—Also Available—

Abide in My Word 2003—Mass Readings at Your Fingertips

Keep abreast with the daily Mass readings and make personal Scripture reading easier! *Abide in My Word* provides each day's Scripture readings in an easy-to-locate format. Each day is clearly listed so that it only takes a few minutes to draw near to the Lord through the Mass readings. Use it together with your prayer journal.

To order, use the card below or call **1-800-775-9673**
You'll find up-to-date product information on our web site at www.wau.org

Fill in the card below and mail in an envelope to:

The Word Among Us
9639 Doctor Perry Road, #126
Ijamsville, MD 21754

Order both books and save $4.50!

- -

☐ **YES!** Send me _____ copies of the **2003 Prayer Journal**   JPRAY3
1 Journal $12.95 plus $4 shipping and handling
2 or more Journals $10.95 each plus $6 S & H

☐ **YES!** Send me _____ copies of **Abide in My Word 2003**   BABDE3
1 Abide in My Word $14.95 plus $5.50 shipping and handling
2 or more books $12.00 each plus $7.50 S & H

☐ **YES!** Send me the 2003 **Prayer Journal** AND 2003 Abide in My Word
for only $26.90 plus $6 shipping and handling   BSET3

Name
_____
Address
_____
City
_____
State _____ Zip _____
Phone (_____)
_____
e-mail (optional)
_____   PJAB3

VISA MasterCard ■ **Send no money now. We will bill you.**